#37

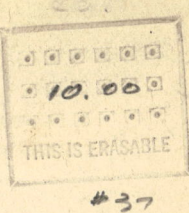

29A

St. Lilac:

When your bright years,
Like stars in night's gemmed splendor,
Have multiplied to constellations
Of the later life that overlook
The petty hilltops of this underworld;
When your clean eyes,
Filled with serenity,
Look toward the dawn of dawn;
When, by the weights that weigh the worlds,
You test the fair philosophies herein —
Shall you not say: The tender love
Bestowing this poor gift
Outweighs the sage's song,
And, by one pulsebeat, finds
The way to happiness
That lies through loving service?

B.H.

12/25/1909.

*Rena L. Hamilton,
"The Lilacs". from Burritt Hamilton.
Nineteen hundred and nine.*

THE LAND OF LONG AGO

"'HERE'S A PICTURE O' HENRIETTA'S HOUSE, CHILD'"
FRONTISPIECE, *See Page* 119.

The Land of Long Ago

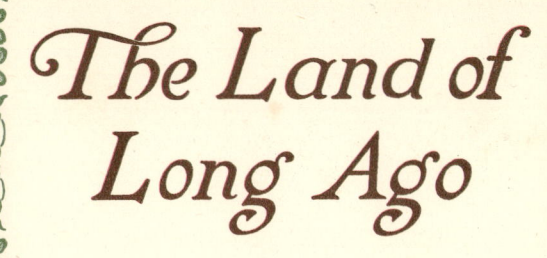

By
Eliza Calvert Hall
Author of
"Aunt Jane of Kentucky"

Illustrated by
G. Patrick Nelson
&
Beulah Strong

Boston
Little, Brown, & Company
1909

Copyright, 1907, 1908, 1909,
BY COSMOPOLITAN PUBLISHING COMPANY.

Copyright, 1909,
BY LITTLE, BROWN, AND COMPANY.

———

All rights reserved

Published, September, 1909

Printers
S. J. PARKHILL & CO., BOSTON, U. S. A.

TO
My Children,
MARGERY, ALEXANDER, THOMAS, AND CECILIA,
I Dedicate this Book

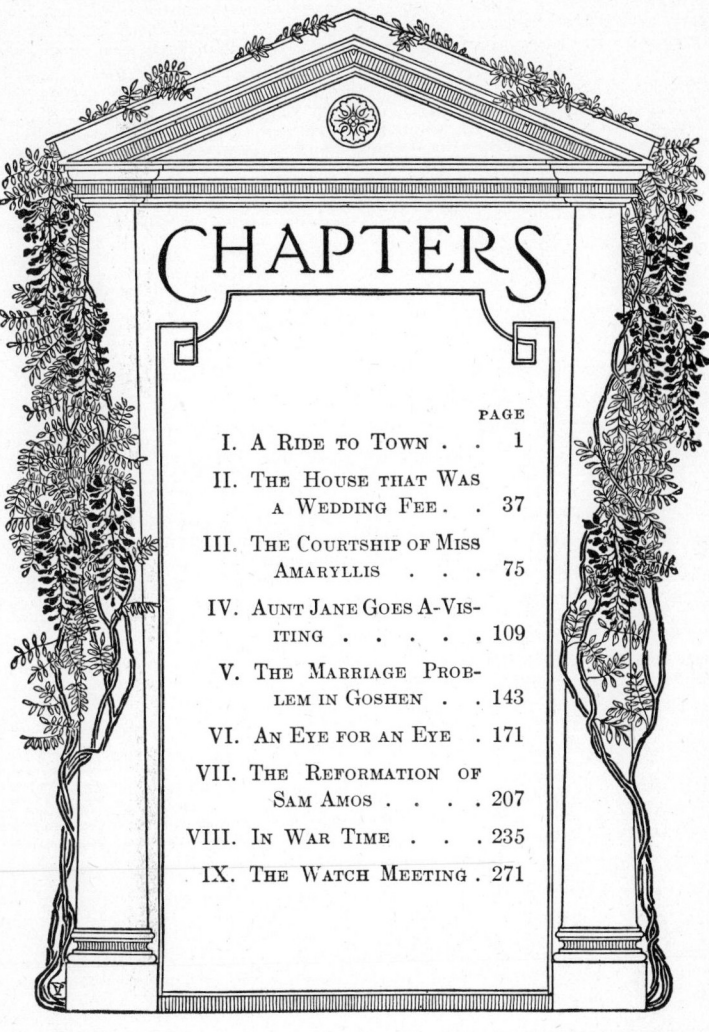

CHAPTERS

		PAGE
I.	A Ride to Town	1
II.	The House that Was a Wedding Fee	37
III.	The Courtship of Miss Amaryllis	75
IV.	Aunt Jane Goes A-Visiting	109
V.	The Marriage Problem in Goshen	143
VI.	An Eye for an Eye	171
VII.	The Reformation of Sam Amos	207
VIII.	In War Time	235
IX.	The Watch Meeting	271

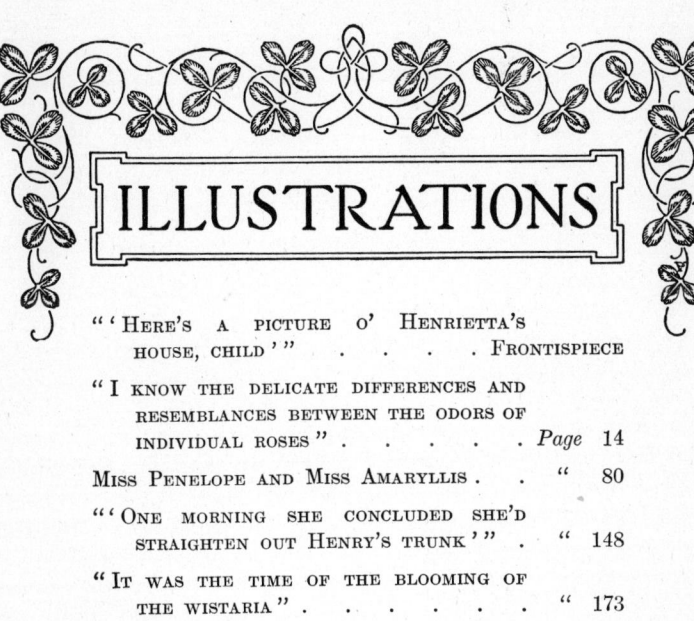

ILLUSTRATIONS

"'Here's a picture o' Henrietta's house, child'" . . . . Frontispiece

"I know the delicate differences and resemblances between the odors of individual roses" . . . . . *Page* 14

Miss Penelope and Miss Amaryllis . . " 80

"'One morning she concluded she'd straighten out Henry's trunk'" . " 148

"It was the time of the blooming of the wistaria" . . . . . . " 173

"'The glass broke into a hundred pieces'" . . . . " 229

"'David! Jonathan! My boys! Where are you?'" . . . . . . " 257

"Reverently she laid the heavy calf-bound volume across her knees" . " 290

PROLOGUE

*We are so near to those who dwell
In the dear land whereof I tell!
Sometimes when we are far astray,
Their spirit-hands may guide our way;
And if we would but pause to hear,
What whispered words of tender cheer
Might come on those fine airs that blow
From the strange Land of Long Ago!*

*The scenes are changed, but we and they
Are actors in the same old play.
Their blood is in our throbbing veins;
Their hopes and joys, their griefs and pains,
Bind us fore'er to squire or churl,
To stately dame or laughing girl,—
Those shades that wander to and fro
In the dim Land of Long Ago.*

*Then let the present hour go by.
Turn back awhile, and you and I
Through quiet garden paths may stray
Where blooms the rose of yesterday,*

PROLOGUE

May meet brave men and women fair
Who sang life's song to simple air;
Mark how their homely virtues glow!—
O pleasant Land of Long Ago!

I
A RIDE TO TOWN

I

A RIDE TO TOWN

"MAKE haste, child," called Aunt Jane; "there's mighty little time between dinner and sundown, and if we're goin' to town we'd better be startin'."

Aunt Jane came out of the house, drawing on a pair of silk gloves. She was arrayed in her best gown of black alpaca, a silk-fringed cape covered her shoulders, her poke bonnet was draped with a veil of

THE LAND OF LONG AGO

figured lace, and under the lace her face shone with happy anticipation, for a lifetime of trips to town had not dulled her enjoyment of such an event.

The horse and buggy stood at the gate. The former had a pedigree as long as that of the penniless lass, and Aunt Jane could tell many wonderful tales of Nelly's spirit and speed in the days of her youth. Some remnant of this fire was supposed to smolder yet in the old thoroughbred, but as I looked at the drooping head and half-shut eyes, I saw there was good reason for Aunt Jane's haste, if we were expected to get back from town before nightfall.

"What are we going to town for?" I asked, as I stepped into the buggy and took up the reins.

Aunt Jane hesitated. "Well," she said, "I'm goin' to lay in a supply o' soda and cream o' tartar, and I may buy some gyarden seed and one thing or another. I ain't exactly out o' soda and cream o' tartar, and I could git the seed from some o' the neighbors. I reckon if the truth was told, I'm goin' to town jest to be a-goin'."

A certain English humorist, who is not so well known to this generation as Mark Twain, once wrote a page of gentle satire about those misguided people who leave their native land to travel in foreign countries. He

A RIDE TO TOWN

finds but three reasons for their folly: "infirmity of body, imbecility of mind, and inevitable necessity"; and the whole circle of such travelers he classifies under the following heads: the Idle, the Inquisitive, the Lying, the Proud, the Vain, and the Splenetic. Had he gone a little farther into his subject, he might have written approvingly of the Innocent Traveler, who, on a May day, sets forth to go from his home in the country to the near-by town, all for the mere pleasure of traveling.

Why, indeed, should the desire for travel send one across oceans or over continents? Wherever we go we find only the old earth and the old sky, and, under varying forms of dress and complexion, the same old humanity of which we are a part. Does not the sun rise or set as splendidly over some blue Kentucky hill as over the Jungfrau? Is the daisy on Mars Hill any fairer than the daisy that opens its petals on any meadow of the New World? And if historic associations are the aim of your wanderings, turn the pages of some old school history, or send your memory on a backward pilgrimage to the olden days, and a country road may carry you into a past as glorious as that which lies along the Appian Way.

THE LAND OF LONG AGO

For a long time we rode in silence. On crowded streets and in towns one must talk; but out of doors in the country there is a Voice continually speaking in a language as old as the song of the morning stars, and if the soul hears that, human words are not needed.

Aunt Jane was the first to speak. "Ain't it sweet and peaceful this time o' the year!" she said. "I look at these pretty fields and woods all fenced in, with good roads runnin' alongside, and it don't seem like it could be jest a little more'n two generations between now and the time when this was the Dark and Bloody Ground, and the white men was fightin' with Indians and bears and wildcats to git possession of it. Why, right over there on that ridge o' hills is the place where Sam Amos's grandfather run the ga'ntlet when he was captured by the Indians. Sam used to have the old tow-linen shirt with the bloodstains and the cut on the shoulder where one o' the Indians struck him with a tomahawk. I ricollect Parson Page used to say that life was jest a runnin' of the ga'ntlet. There's enemies on each side of us, and every one of 'em is strikin' at us. And we can't run away, and we know that there's one stroke comin' some time or other that's certain to bring us down.

A RIDE TO TOWN

And all we've got to do is to stand up and keep goin' right on, and be ready for the last blow, whenever it happens to fall. And here's Devil's Holler," she continued; "look down that bluff, and you'll see it."

I looked and saw a deep cup-shaped valley, dark with the shadows of overhanging rocks and trees, and luxuriant with ferns and underbrush that grew rankly out of soil made rich by the drifted leaves of a hundred autumns.

"Some folks say that the old stage road used to run past here, and a band o' robbers used to hide by the side o' the road and waylay the stage and rob the passengers, and maybe murder 'em and bury their bodies at the bottom o' the holler. And "—she lowered her voice—"some folks say the place is ha'nted. Sam Amos declared the devil come out o' that holler and chased him for half a mile one dark night when he was late comin' home from town. But I reckon the only devil that chased Sam was the devil in the bottom of his whiskey-jug, and Uncle Billy Bascom says there never was any stage line along this road within his ricollection. So there you are; don't know what to believe and what not to believe."

Just here the road made a steep, upward curve,

THE LAND OF LONG AGO

and we looked down on the clear, green ripples of a river that wound between high rocky cliffs on one hand, and on the other vast fields of corn growing lustily in the deep, rich soil.

"Why should such a pretty little river be called the Barren River?" I asked. "There isn't anything barren about the river or the country around it."

Aunt Jane's eyes sparkled. She was capable of answering the question, for it touched a page of ancient history that was to her a twice-told tale. "You see all these trees, child?" she said impressively, waving her hand in the direction of the luxuriant masses of foliage. "Jest look at that tulip-tree yonder, eighty feet high, I reckon, and the flowers standin' up all over it like the gold candlesticks the Bible tells about. You wouldn't think all these trees could grow up since the first settlers come through here. But I've heard father tell about it many a time. He said the Indians used to set fire to the woods and the fields, and when the first settlers come through here, they called this the Barrens on account o' there bein' no trees, and they passed by all this good land and went further up on Gasper River, where there was springs comin' out o' the hills and plenty of trees. You see, there's two things a

A RIDE TO TOWN

settler has to have: wood and water; and that's why the country up around Gasper was settled before this was, and this got the name of the Barrens, when there ain't a richer lot o' ground anywhere.

"And speakin' of names, honey, did I ever tell you how Kittle Creek got its name?

"Well, now, folks has been laughin' about that story for the last seventy-five years, and I reckon they'll keep on laughin' as long as there's a old man or a old woman like me livin' to tell it;" and Aunt Jane began laughing in advance of the story.

"The right name o' Kittle Creek is Clear Fork," she said, "but it's been Kittle Creek ever since old man Sam Stapleton give it that name. And this was the way of it. Old man Sam lived on the fur side o' the creek, and he was in the habit o' comin' to town every once in a while to lay in his groceries and such things, and every time he'd come to town he'd git his jug filled, of course, and drink all along the way home; but by the time he'd git to Clear Fork he wouldn't know where he was, or who he was, or which way he was goin'. He was a mighty good-hearted man, but that jug was his besettin' sin.

"Well, one evenin' he was comin' home the usual

THE LAND OF LONG AGO

way, him and the jug, and he got to the creek and concluded he'd git off his horse and lay down and take a little nap. Some o' the women folks in that neighborhood had been doin' their washin' that day, and there was a big iron kittle on the bank set up on some stones where they'd b'iled their clothes. Old man Sam laid down by the kittle and went to sleep. Pretty soon he got awake and set up and rubbed his eyes, and took notice of the kittle, and says he,

" 'Have I crossed this creek or not?' says he. 'It appears to me like I've seen this kittle before, but whether it was on this side o' the creek or the other, to save my life I can't tell.'

" Then he studied a while and says he,

" 'Well, I'll give myself the benefit of the doubt.' So he crossed the creek, got off his horse and set down in the shade, and took a drink out o' the jug and fell asleep again. After a while he woke up and looked around, and says he: 'Here I am again, and here's the creek, and yonder's that old kittle jest as natural as life. But what I want to know is, am I agoin' to town, or am I comin' back home?' And he looked at the sun, and says he, 'Judgin' by the way that sun looks, it might be nine o'clock in the mornin', and it

A RIDE TO TOWN

might be three o'clock in the evenin'; and not bein' a Solomon I ain't able to decide which it is, but I'll take my chances and go across the creek.'

"So across the creek he went, took another drink, and laid down and fell asleep right by the kittle. Pretty soon he woke up the third time, and says he: 'Well, if here ain't that old kittle again! Howdy, Mr. Kittle! Can you tell me which way I'm goin', and whether it's mornin' or evenin'?'

"Well, the kittle didn't answer; and the old man set there and thought a while, and then he crossed the creek and took another drink and another nap, and crossed again, and there was the same old kittle, and he looked at it and give it a kick, and says he: 'I never saw as many blame kittles in all my life as I've seen to-day. I reckon this must be Kittle Creek.'"

Aunt Jane paused to join in my laughter.

"I always thought it was a shame to laugh at a poor drunkard," she resumed, "but old man Sam told the Kittle Creek story on himself. I don't reckon he thought he was changin' the name of Clear Fork Creek, but from that time on nobody ever called it anything but Kittle Creek."

She stopped and peered over the side of the buggy.

THE LAND OF LONG AGO

Her keen eyes had detected a change in the road. There had been no rain for a week, but the horse's hoofs and the wheels of our buggy had suddenly ceased to raise any dust.

"Looks like there'd been a shower here lately," she remarked; "but I don't see any sign o' rain except right here in the middle o' the road."

"Perhaps this is the oiled road, Aunt Jane," said I.

"That's jest what it is!" exclaimed Aunt Jane delightedly. "Uncle Billy Bascom was tellin' me about the new-fangled way they had of layin' the dust, but it didn't seem to me like oil'd mix with dust any more'n it will with water. That shows how little old folks knows. Well, ain't this nice! Ridin' along in dry weather and never raisin' a bit o' dust! Uncle Billy didn't approve o' the oiled roads. He says, says he, 'Jane, it looks to me like them town folks won't never git through circumventin' Providence.' Says he, 'They've got their gas and their 'lectricity, so's it don't make a bit o' difference whether the sun or the moon or the stars shines or not. And they've got their 'lectric fans, which makes 'em independent of the wind blowin', and now they're fixin' the roads so's they won't have to pray for rain.' Says he, 'It looks

A RIDE TO TOWN

like they're tryin' to git rid of all sense o' dependence on the Almighty; but as for me,' says he, ' I've got my pegs sot, and I ain't goin' to have my brains all tore up follerin' after new ways.'

"That's jest like Uncle Billy. But all the time I'm ridin' along this road I'm feelin' thankful to Providence that he made the oil, and then made people with enough sense to know that oil would settle dust. There's no use stickin' to old ways unless they're better than the new ways."

Just then there was a whir of wings from a fence corner, and a moment later a liquid voice sounded over the clover field,

Bob White, is your wheat ripe?

Most birds have a song of but one season. The bluebird, for instance, sings only of spring; but in the two simple notes of the partridge there is the melody of falling water, a song of April's pale-green fields, a song of summer's golden grain, and another of autumn's scarlet leaf and frosty morning.

"That's a voice that won't be heard in the land much longer," remarked Aunt Jane; "and when it does stop, it'll be like missin' a voice from the church

THE LAND OF LONG AGO

choir. The wild things are disappearin' one by one. The deer's all gone, and even squirrels are gittin' so skeerce the legislature'll have to pass a law to protect 'em. And I'm bound to say the first settlers is a good deal to blame for it all. Game was so plentiful in them early days that nobody thought about it ever givin' out. Every man was a hunter — he had to be to provide his family with meat — and I've heard father say that every boy in them days was born with a gun in his hand. Old Jonathan Petty, Silas's father, had nine sons, all of 'em sharpshooters. They used to shoot at squirrels for a mark, and if they hit the squirrel anywhere but in the head, old Jonathan'd give 'em a good whippin'. That sort o' trainin' was bound to make a boy a good marksman, but it was hard on the squirrels."

I had thought myself deeply learned in the lore of sweet odors. I know that the orient spells of sandalwood can intoxicate like the opium-pipe or the draught of Indian hemp. I know the delicate differences and resemblances between the odors of individual roses. I know that when nature made the coarse hollyhock, she gave it the almond perfume that floats over the waves of the Hellespont from the petals of the patrician

A RIDE TO TOWN

oleander growing on its banks. And I know that, in the same mood, she dowered the vulgar horseweed with the breath of the mignonette. Every odor is to me as a note of music, and I know the discords and harmonies in the long, long scale of perfume. I know that heliotrope and mignonette make a dissonance, and heliotrope and tea-roses a perfect third; that there is a chord of melody in heliotrope, tea-roses, and honeysuckle; and in the orange-blossom or tuberose a dominant note that is stronger than any symphony of perfume that can be composed from summer's garden-beds. There are perfumes as evanescent as the dreams of youth, and others as persistent as the memories of childhood. Go into the fields in February, gather the dead pennyroyal that has stood through the rains and snows of a long winter, and you will find in its dry stems and shriveled leaves the same gracious scent the green plant has in June. A rose of last October is a poor deflowered thing; but turn to the ice-bound garden-walks where, a month before, the chrysanthemum stood in autumn splendor. The beautiful acanthus-like leaves and the once gorgeous blossoms hang in brown tatters, but still they hold the perfume of lavender and camphor, and from autumn to spring the plant stands embalmed in its own sweetness, like the body of a mummied Pharaoh wrapped in precious gums and spices. I know that the flowers called scentless have their hours when the spirit of perfume visits them and lends them, for a brief season, the charm without which a flower is only half a flower. I have found the fragrance of ripe cherries in the wood of the cherry parted a lifetime from the parent tree. I have marveled over the alchemy that gives to the bitter shriveled fruit of the wild crab-apple tree a fragrance as sweet as its blossom. The heart of a child beats in me at the scent of a green walnut or a handful of fresh hickory leaves; and I have cried out for words to express what I feel when the incense of the wild grape blossom rises from the woodland altars of late spring, and I stand, a lonely worshiper, at a shrine deserted " since the old Hellenic days." But what was that breath coming across the meadows on the sun-warmed air? Was it a lost breeze from the Indian Ocean, caught in some gulf-stream of the air and drifted down into the wind-currents that blow across Kentucky fields in May?

"Strawberries, strawberries, child," said Aunt Jane. " Didn't you ever smell strawberries when the evenin' sun's shinin' on 'em and ripenin' 'em, and the wind's

A RIDE TO TOWN

blowin' over 'em like it's blowin' now? There's a ten-acre patch o' strawberries jest across that medder."

It was impossible to go on while that perfume came and went like a far-off, exquisite voice, and even Aunt Jane forgot her hurry to get to town, as we sat with our faces eagerly turned toward the unseen field of strawberries.

"I've heard folks say," said Aunt Jane, "that Kentucky is the natural home o' the strawberry, and I reckon it's so, for I ricollect how, when I was a child, the strawberries grew wild in the pastures, and the cows'd come home at night with their hoofs dyed red with the juice o' the berries they'd been treadin' on all day. Parson Page used to say there was some things that showed the goodness of the Lord, and some things, such as strawberries and grapes and apples and peaches, that showed the exceeding great goodness of the Lord. He'd never eat a strawberry without first holdin' it up and lookin' at it and smellin' it, and he'd say:

"'Now wouldn't you think it was enough to have a strawberry tastin' like it does? But here it is, the prettiest color in the world, pretty as any rose, and, besides that, smellin' like the sweetest flower that grows.' "

" What is the sweetest flower that grows ? " I asked.

" Don't ask me such a question as that," said Aunt Jane with emphasis. " Every one's the sweetest while I'm smellin' it. But when Parson Page talked about the sweetest flower, he meant the calycanthus. There's mighty little difference between smellin' a bowl o' strawberries and a handful o' calycanthuses. Yes, the world's full o' sweet things, child, and you don't have to look in gyardens to find 'em, either. They're scattered around everywhere and free for everybody. Jest look yonder in that old fence corner. There's catnip and hoarhound and horsemint and pennyroy'l, and pretty soon there'll be wild life-everlastin'. Yes, it's a mighty sweet world. I'm glad I've lived in it this long, and heaven'll have to be somethin' mighty fine if it's any better'n this old earth. Now hurry up, child, or we won't have time to see the town sights before dark comes."

Within a mile of town I noticed a house barely visible at the end of an avenue so long that it made me think of the " lane that knows no turning."

" What house is that ? " I asked.

A RIDE TO TOWN

Aunt Jane's eyes twinkled. "That's the house that was a weddin' fee," she said mysteriously.

"A wedding fee?" I echoed doubtfully.

"A weddin' fee," repeated Aunt Jane. "But don't ask me any questions about it now, for there ain't time to tell it before we git to town."

"But you'll tell it on the way back?" I urged eagerly.

"Yes, child, yes. But hurry up now. I don't believe you care whether we git to town or not."

I shook the lines over Nelly's back, tapped her gently with the whip, and on we went. Aunt Jane was impatient to get to town, but I — I wished for a longer road, a slower steed, and a Joshua to command the afternoon sun to stand still a while in the heavens. For it was the last day of May. Time stood reluctant on the border line between spring and summer, and in every bird-song and every whisper of the wind I seemed to hear,

"Farewell, farewell, to another spring!"

"You see that pretty farm yonder?" said Aunt Jane, pointing to the left. "Fields as level as a parlor floor and soil like a river-bottom? That farm belonged to Henry Amos, Sam Amos's youngest brother. Henry

THE LAND OF LONG AGO

got the gold-fever back in '49, him and a lot of other young fellers, and nothin' would do but he must go to California. And here's Henry's farm, but where Henry is nobody knows. Every time I see the yeller wheat standin' in these fields, I think of how Henry's grandfather begged him not to go. Henry was his favorite grandchild, and it broke the old man's heart to see him leave. He took hold o' Henry's hand and led him to the front door and says he,

"'Son, do you think the Lord was so forgetful of his children as to put all the gold in the world out yonder in California?' Says he, 'That potato-patch over there is a gold-mine, and there's a gold-mine in that wheat-field, and another one in the corn-field. And if you'll go down in the orchard and gether a load o' them pippin apples and a few punkins, and haul 'em to town and sell 'em, you'll find there's some gold in them.' Says he, 'The whole earth's a gold-mine, if men jest have the patience to dig it out.' But Henry would go, and I reckon he couldn't help it, poor boy! Some folks are born to stay at home, and some are born with the wanderin' fever in their bones."

I looked at the fertile fields that were the dead man's heritage, and read again the old story of restless human

A RIDE TO TOWN

ambition that loses the near and the familiar by grasping at the far-off and unknown.

We were nearing the town limits now. Instead of the infrequent farmhouses, we were passing rows of pretty suburban homes. Now and then a fine old elm by the roadside, or within some neat, flowery yard, spoke of the "forest primeval" vanishing before the stealthy march of a growing town.

Aunt Jane's face wore the look of the pilgrim who approaches the City Beautiful. She loved the country, and nature had kindly given her the power to love one thing without hating its antithesis. But, apart from Aunt Jane's company, going to town had no attraction for me, to whom a town is only one of those necessary evils whose sum total we call civilization. And while Aunt Jane took delighted notice of the street-cars, the newly laid concrete walks, the sprinkling-cart, and the automobile with its discordant warning voice, my heart turned back regretfully to the narrow wayside path bordered by dusty weeds and watered only by the dew and rain, to the old "dirt road," marked by the track of the lazy ox-team or the two-horse wagon, and hushed and bounded by the great silences of field and wood.

THE LAND OF LONG AGO

Aunt Jane was smiling and looking to right and left, and the children on the street were quick to respond with answering smiles, as the kind old face beamed on them. Chauffeurs and drivers of stylish carriages politely gave us the road, and so we jogged into the little square, the heart of the town. The park was in its spring raiment of young leaves and grass, and the waters of the fountain sparkled in the sunshine.

"It's the prettiest little town in the State," said Aunt Jane proudly.

"Where shall we go first?" I asked.

"There's one place in this town where all us country folks goes first," said Aunt Jane oracularly, "and that's the old drug-store on the corner yonder. Let the mare alone, and she'll go right there without guidin'."

And so she did, stopping at a corner of the square before a three-story brick building with none of the usual signs of a drug-store about it. Aunt Jane stepped out to make her purchases, and I stayed in the buggy to hold the horse, an unnecessary precaution, for old Nelly at once dropped her head in a drowsy, meditative way that showed she had no intention of leaving the familiar stopping-place.

A RIDE TO TOWN

I heard a cheery voice within giving Aunt Jane an old friend's greeting, and while she made her purchases and gossiped with the proprietor over the high, old-fashioned counter, I stared into the dark, dingy vista of the ancient store. The stone door-step, hollowed like the steps to the Blarney stone, had borne the steady tread of feet for sixty years, and the floor within was worn in the same way. At the far end of the store, I discerned a group of elderly men. Some were seated on packing-boxes, conveniently placed around the store for the use of those who desired to stay a while to rest and whittle; others reposed on the small of their backs in rickety, splint-bottomed chairs tilted against the wall, their feet on the rounds of the chairs, their knees on a level with their chins, and about them an air of profound repose that showed them to be as much a part of the store as the old iron stove. The window proclaimed the place the den of an archæologist, for it was filled with arrow-heads neatly mounted on pasteboard, Indian pottery, petrifactions, stone hammers, tomahawks, relics of aboriginal and prehistoric man that the mounds and caves of Kentucky yield up to the seeker of such buried treasure. Both within and without, the old store was like an embodiment of conservatism standing unmoved while the swift currents of modern progress were sweeping around it and beating against it.

While I was gazing and wondering, Aunt Jane came out. "I reckon you think this is a curious-lookin' place, honey," she said, as she stowed away her packages on the seat. "This old store is one o' the places that ain't changed in my memory. 'Stablished in 1847, and I don't reckon it's had a right good cleanin' from that day to this, but the best of everything a drug-store keeps is in them old dusty bottles and jars. It does me good to come to town and find one place lookin' jest like it did when me and Abram used to come on county-court days and circus days. And there's the old men sittin' around that stove. They've been there for the last twenty-five years, and they'll be there till death comes along and picks 'em up and carries 'em away. And now, child, give me the lines. I'm goin' to drive around a little while, and then we'll go home."

She took the lines and began what seemed to me an aimless ramble through the streets of the town. She grew strangely silent, and that look on her face — was it sadness or only joy in retrospect? I began to see the

A RIDE TO TOWN

meaning of our ride to town. The garden-seed and other purchases were but a vain pretext. In reality, she had come to keep a tryst with the past. Now and then she remembered my presence, and would point to some place that was a link between to-day and yesterday. Here was the place in which General Buckner had made his headquarters during the Civil War; in that house Charles Sumner was once a guest; on yonder height stood a Confederate fortification, and on a similar elevation on the opposite side of town was another fort erected by a Federal commander, afterward a president; and — wondrous miracle! — the angel of peace had turned the old fort into a garden. As Aunt Jane spoke, the light of other days shone for me, too, and in its radiance the commonplace faded out of sight.

We traveled in a circle, and our ride ended where it had begun. As we paused at the drinking-fountain to let old Nelly quench her thirst, Aunt Jane leaned out of the buggy and looked wistfully up and down the square. I knew what was in her heart. She was thinking that, perhaps, this was the last time she would see the town.

"It's a curious thing, child," she said finally, "that while folks are growin' old, the towns they live in are growin' young. The town I ricollect when I was a young gyirl is the old town, and now, when I'm old, the town's young, and growin' younger and newer every day. Ain't it a pity folks can't grow young instead of growin' old?" She paused, and I felt the distance of a lifetime growing up between us.

Presently she came out of her reverie, smiling brightly. "We're lookin' at the same things, honey," she said, "but you see jest one thing, and I'm seein' double all the time. You see this square with the park in the middle and the fine four- and five-story buildin's all around it, and I see it, too; but back of it I can see the old square with the court-house in the middle of it and the scraggly locust-trees growin' around it and the market-house back of it. That market-house wasn't much to look at, but the meat they sold there was the sort a king can't git nowadays. And there was the clerk's office in front of the court-house, and the county clerk used to stand on the door-step and call out the names of the witnesses that was wanted when they was tryin' a case in court. I can see him now, holdin' up a piece o' paper to read the names off, and the sun shinin' on his gray head. And that three-story hotel over yonder on the corner — that used to be

A RIDE TO TOWN

the old tavern in the days when there wasn't any railroad, and the stage'd come rumblin' up, and everybody'd come runnin' to their front doors to see who the passengers was.

"The town was so quiet in them days, child, that you could lay down in the court-house yard and go to sleep, and so little that if you put your head out o' the winder and hollered for John Smith, you'd be pretty certain to git John Smith. If he didn't hear you, some of his neighbors would, and they'd hunt him up for you. Things wasn't as well kept then as they are now. I ricollect the jimson-weeds growin' in the court-house yard, and one year the dog-fennel was so plentiful that Uncle Jim Matthews says to me, says he, 'It looks to me like the Smiths and the Joneses and the dog-fennel are about to take the town.'"

She laughed gaily and handed the reins to me. "And now, child, we've got to make tracks for home, unless we want to be out after sundown."

As we passed out of the square, our faces turned homeward, I noticed an old Gothic church on the corner of the street leading to the court-house.

"There's another thing that ain't changed much," said Aunt Jane, with great satisfaction in her voice.

THE LAND OF LONG AGO

"The inside's all new, and there's a new congregation, for all the old congregation's lyin' out in the new cemetery or the old graveyard. But there's the same walls standin' and lookin' jest like they did when I used to come to town with father and mother. Makes me think of a body with a new soul in it. Wonder if the old bell's still up yonder in the steeple.

"Speakin' o' that bell reminds me o' Martin Luther Wilson and the time he kept it from ringin'. Now, wait till we're fairly outside o' town, and I'll tell you about it."

When all signs of town were fully half a mile behind us the story began.

"That church you saw back yonder, honey," she said, "was built when the Rev. Samuel Wilson was the pastor, and as soon as it was done and the bell put up in the belfry, Brother Wilson said that bell had to ring every Saturday mornin' to call the children of the congregation together in the basement o' the church to receive religious instruction. He'd been visitin' amongst the church-members, and he'd found out that some o' the children didn't know the Ten Commandments or the Shorter Catechism or the Lord's Prayer, and when he asked one child what a foreign missionary was, the little thing thought a minute and says she,

A RIDE TO TOWN

'Why, it's a rabbit, ain't it?' Well, of course Brother Wilson was clean scandalized, and says he, 'Such a state of things is a disgrace to a civilized community. And,' says he, 'if the parents of the church haven't got time to instruct their children, I'll do it myself, for it's part of my pastoral duty to feed the lambs of this flock as well as the sheep.'

"Well, of course the parents had no objection to havin' the children taught. I ricollect old Mis' Zerilda Moore said that if Brother Wilson could teach her boy Joe to say the Ten Commandments, he was welcome to the job, for all her time was taken up tryin' to git Joe to keep a few of 'em. The little gyirls didn't mind goin' to Saturday-mornin' Sunday School, as they called it, but the boys objected mightily, especially Brother Wilson's boys, Martin Luther and John Calvin. And Martin Luther says, says he, 'It ain't fair to take a lamb's play-time away from it to feed it on such fodder as that Shorter Catechism.' Says he, 'Any healthy lamb can stand the Ten Commandments and the Lord's Prayer; I can say 'em frontwards and backwards myself, but,' says he, 'when it comes to the catechism, there'll be some lambs missin' from this flock when Saturday mornin' comes.'

THE LAND OF LONG AGO

"Well, one mornin' not long after this, the old sexton went to ring the bell for the children to come to the church, and he pulled the rope and pulled the rope and couldn't make a sound; and while he was standin' lookin' up in the belfry and pullin' and wonderin', here come Brother Wilson wantin' to know why that bell hadn't been rung. Brother Wilson was a man that was always on time himself, and he hadn't any patience with folks that wasn't.

"And old Uncle Gloster says, 'Boss, I'm doin' my best, but it looks like somebody's done hoodooed this bell.' Says he, 'I'm jest gittin' over a spell o' rheumatism, and my old j'ints won't stand a climb up that ladder, and you'll have to git somebody that's young and spry to go up and see what's the matter.'

"Well, Brother Wilson started off to find somebody who could climb the ladder, and as soon as he got outside the church, he met Judge Grace and old Doctor Brigham, both of 'em members of the church, and he told 'em about the trouble with the bell, and they went in to see what they could do. By the time Brother Wilson had walked around the square, everybody in town knew that the Presbyterian bell wouldn't ring, and all the folks come flockin' to the church; but no-

A RIDE TO TOWN

body wanted to risk their neck goin' up the old rickety ladder. While they was all standin' there stretchin' their necks and reckonin' about what was the matter, here come John Calvin, and says he, 'Gimme fifty cents, and I'll go up the ladder.'

"And Brother Wilson says, 'No child o' mine shall be hired to do his duty.' Says he, 'John Calvin, if that ladder was a green-apple tree, you'd be at the top of it in less than half a minute. Go up, sir, this instant, and find out what's the matter with that bell.'

"But Judge Grace and Doctor Brigham and the rest o' the men said they'd throw in and make up the fifty cents, and John Calvin put the money in his pocket and went up the ladder. As soon as he got to the top round he hollered down and says he:

"'No wonder the bell won't ring. Here's a yarn sock tied around the clapper.' And down he come with the sock in his hand, and handed it to his father. It turned out afterwards that him and Martin Luther had had a fallin' out that mornin', and he went up and got the sock jest to git even with his brother.

"Well, while they was passin' the sock around and speculatin' about it, old Mis' Maria Morris come along with her bag o' knittin' on her arm, goin' to spend the

THE LAND OF LONG AGO

day with some of her friends. She stopped to see what was the matter, and when they told her she says, 'Let me look at the sock,' and she took it and looked at it right close and says she, 'That's Martin Luther Wilson's sock,' says she. 'I spent the day with Mis' Wilson three or four weeks ago, and I saw her round off the toe of this very sock.'

"Well, of course, Brother Wilson started off to look for Martin Luther, and as soon as he was out o' hearin', Judge Grace brought his cane down on the pavement, and says he, 'I hate to say such a thing of my own pastor's son, but they named that boy after the wrong man when they named him Martin Luther,' says he. 'They ought to 'a' named him Beelzebub. That's one good old Bible name,' says he, 'that'll fit a preacher's son nine times out of ten.'

"Brother Wilson went all around the square inquirin' for Martin Luther, and found out that Martin and the rest o' the boys had been seen goin' towards the river, all of 'em bleatin' like young lambs callin' for their mothers. So he come back to the church, and says he to Judge Grace, 'What mortifies me most in this matter is that a boy of mine should have so little sense as to tie his own sock on the bell. It was

A RIDE TO TOWN

the act of a fool,' says he, ' and I shall see that it is properly punished.'

"So when Martin Luther got home late that evenin', his mother was standin' on the front door-step waitin' for him, and she took him by the hand and led him into his father's study. And Brother Wilson held up the sock, and says he, ' My son, can you tell me how this came to be tied on the clapper of the church bell?' And Martin Luther says, as prompt as you please, ' Yes, sir; I tied it on myself.' Martin's mother said Brother Wilson looked mighty pleased at that. And then he says, ' Well, didn't you know you'd be found out if you tied your own sock on?' And Martin Luther says, ' Yes, but I had to take my chances on that, for if I'd gone home to git a rag or anything like that, Uncle Gloster might 'a' had the church locked up before I could git back.' Mis' Wilson used to say that Brother Wilson laughed like he'd heard good news when Martin Luther said that, and says he, ' Well, I'm glad to know you are neither a liar nor a fool, but, all the same, I shall have to correct you severely for this offense.'

"Brother Wilson believed in Solomon's plan for raisin' children, and in them days preachers didn't try to explain away the meanin' of a Bible text like they do now. So he give Martin Luther a good old-fashioned whippin', and then he called for John Calvin, and says he, 'I know you were as deep in the mud as your brother was in the mire, and I understand now why you were so anxious to climb the ladder and see what was the matter with the bell: you only wanted to get your brother into trouble, so I shall give you a double punishment.'

"And besides the whippin', Martin Luther said they made him and John Calvin learn pretty near all the psalms. That's the way children was dealt with in old times. Martin Luther used to say, 'Boys, if I got all this for tyin' one sock on that old bell-clapper, what would it 'a' been if I'd tied a pair o' socks on it?'"

The old farmhouse was in sight, and Nelly's brisk gait showed what she could do if she would. Such inspiration is the thought of home, even to dumb animals. Suddenly I drew rein and assumed a look of deep dismay.

"Aunt Jane," I cried, "we have forgotten something."

"La, child, you don't say so," said Aunt Jane, turning over the parcels in her lap and hurriedly counting

A RIDE TO TOWN

them. "Why, no we ain't. Here's the soda and the cream o' tartar and the gyarden seed all right."

"But you forgot to tell me the story of the house that was a wedding fee," said I with dramatic solemnity.

"Now did anybody ever!" laughed Aunt Jane. "Skeerin' me to death about a old yarn like that! Well, honey, that story's sixty years old already, and I reckon it'll keep a little longer yet. Some o' these days I'll tell you the story of that old house. I reckon I owe you another story for takin' me to town and bringin' me home so nice. I'm mighty glad I've seen the old place once more, for the next time I go to town maybe I'll go in the direction of the New Jerusalem."

After Nelly had been unharnessed and fed, I sat down on the porch to watch the passing of day. Ah! surely it is worth while to go to town now and then just for the pleasure of getting back to the country, to its purer air, its solitude, its blessed stillness. I lifted up my eyes unto the hills and let the sunset and the twilight hold me in their spells till Aunt Jane's voice called me in with a warning of the danger that lurks in falling dew; and when I closed my eyes in sleep that night, my brain was a panorama of strange scenes. Past and present were mingled, as a picture painted

THE LAND OF LONG AGO

within a picture, for, through Aunt Jane's eyes, I, too, had seen double. I had gone to town over the old 'pike, but I had also traveled the road of dead years, and it had led me into the Land of Long Ago.

II
THE HOUSE THAT WAS A WEDDING FEE

II

THE HOUSE THAT WAS A WEDDING FEE

IT was September, the sad month of the year before I heard the promised story of the house that was a wedding fee; for it was Aunt Jane's whim that, as a dramatic sequence, a visit to the house should follow the telling of the tale, and it was hard to find a convenient time for the happening of both events. Meanwhile, I was tantalized by the memory of that half-seen house at the end of the long avenue, and again and again I tried by adroit questions to draw from Aunt Jane the story about which my imagination hovered like a bee about a flower.

"Well," she finally remarked with smiling resignation, "I see there ain't any peace for me till that story's told. Ain't that Johnny Amos goin' by on horseback? Holler to him, child, and ask him to stop here on his way back and hitch old Nelly to the buggy for me. Tell him I'll dance at his weddin' if he'll do that favor for me.

"And now, while we're waitin' for Johnny to come, I'll tell all I can ricollect about that old house. Fetch my basket o' cyarpet-rags, and we'll sit out here on the porch. Here's a needle for you, too, child. If I can sew and talk at the same time, I reckon you can sew and listen. Jest mix your colors any way you please. I never made a cyarpet except the hit-or-miss kind."

I took my needle and began to sew, first a black, then a red, then a blue strip, but Aunt Jane showed no haste to begin her story.

"Goin' back sixty years," she remarked meditatively, "is like goin' up and rummagin' around in a garret. You don't know what you'll lay your hands

HOUSE THAT WAS A WEDDING FEE

on in the dark, and you can't be certain of findin' what you went after. I'm tryin' to think whereabouts I'd better begin so as to git to that old house the quickest."

"No, Aunt Jane, please take the long, roundabout way," I urged.

"Well," she laughed, "come to think about it, it don't make much difference which way I take, for if I start on the short road, it'll be roundabout before I git through with it. You know my failin', child. Well, I reckon the old church is as good a startin'-place as any. You ricollect me p'intin' it out to you the day we went to town, and tellin' you about Martin Luther and the bell. That buildin' was put up when Brother Wilson was pastor of the Presbyterian church. Before his time they'd been without a preacher for a good while, and things was in a run-down and gone-to-seed sort o' condition when he come up from Tennessee to take the charge.

"Brother Wilson's father and mother was Georgia people, and I ricollect one of his brothers comin' through here with all his slaves on his way to Mizzourah to set 'em free. The family moved from Georgia to Tennessee because there was better schools there, and they wanted to educate their children. They was

THE LAND OF LONG AGO

the sort o' people that thought more of books and learnin' than they did of money. But before Brother Wilson got his schoolin', he took a notion he'd go into the army, and when he wasn't but sixteen or seventeen years old, he was fightin' under Gen. Andrew Jackson, and went through two campaigns. Then he come home and went to college, and the next thing he was preachin' the gospel.

"It's sort o' curious to think of a man bein' a soldier and a preacher, too. But then, you know, the Bible talks about Christians jest like they was soldiers, and the Christian's life jest like it was a warfare. The Apostle tells us to put on the whole armor of God, and when he was ready to depart he said, 'I have fought a good fight.' And I used to think that maybe Brother Wilson wouldn't 'a' been as good a preacher as he was if he hadn't first been a good soldier. He used to say, 'I come of fighting stock and preaching stock, and the fighting blood in me had to have its day.' The preachin' blood didn't seem to come out in Martin Luther and John Calvin, but the fightin' blood was there mighty strong. Folks used to say that one or the other of 'em had a fight every day in the week, and if they couldn't git up a fight with some other boy, they'd fight with each other. The druggist said that after Brother Wilson come, he sold as much court-plaster and arnica in a month as he used to sell in six months, and Mis' Zerilda Moore used to declare she never had seen Martin Luther but once when his eyes and nose was the natural shape and color. Some of the church-members was scandalized at havin' their preacher's sons set such a bad example to the rest o' the town boys, and they went to Brother Wilson to talk to him about it. But he jest laughed and says he, 'There's no commandment that says, "Thou shalt not fight," and I can't whip my boys for having the spirit of their forefathers on both sides of the house.' Says he, 'Their great-grandfather on their mother's side was a fighting parson in Revolutionary times. He was in his pulpit one Sunday morning when news was brought that the British were coming, and he stepped down out of his pulpit and organized a company from the men of his congregation, and marched out and whipped the British; and then he went back to the church and finished his sermon.' Says he, 'My boys can't help fighting like their mother's grandfather any more than they can help having their mother's eyes and hair.'

"Now here I am talkin' about Martin Luther

THE LAND OF LONG AGO

Wilson's great-grandfather when I started out to tell you about the old church. Le's see if I can't git back to the straight road and keep on it the rest of the way.

"When Brother Wilson first come, the Presbyterian church was in the old graveyard in the lower part o' town. Maybe you ricollect seein' it the day we went to town. Mighty dismal-lookin' place, all grown up in weeds and underbrush. And he took a look at it and saw jest how things was, and says he, 'You've got your church in the right place. A dead church,' says he, 'ought to be in a graveyard. But,' says he, 'when the spirit of the Lord breathes over this valley of dry bones, I expect to see the dead arise, and we'll build a house of the Lord amongst the habitations of the living.' And bless your life, he went to work and got up a revival that lasted three months, and spread to all the churches — the Babtist and the Methodist and the Christian — till every sinner in town was either converted or at the mourners' bench. And before it was over in town, it started in the country churches and kept up till Sam Amos said it looked to him like the preachers would have to go out o' business for a while or move to some other place, for there wasn't any material in the

HOUSE THAT WAS A WEDDING FEE

county for 'em to work on. Mother used to say it was pretty near equal to the big revival they had 'way back yonder in 1830. She said every seat in a church then was a mourners' bench, and such shoutin' and singin' and prayin' never was heard before or since. Some o' the converts would fall in trances, and you couldn't tell whether they was dead or alive. Uncle Jim Matthews's father, Job Matthews, stayed in a trance for two days and nights, and mother said he never seemed like the same man after that. He never could tell what he'd seen when he was in the trance, and when folks'd question him about it, a sort of a wild look'd come into the old man's eyes and he'd say, ' I've seen things of which it is not lawful for me to speak.' He didn't take any more interest in his farmin' or the family affairs, and when his wife'd try to stir him up and persuade him to work like he'd been used to workin', he'd say: ' The things of this world are temporal, but the things of the other world are eternal. The soul of man is eternal, and this world can never content it. I've seen the abiding-place o' the soul,' he'd say, ' and I'm like a homesick child.' Mother said nobody appeared to understand the old man, and his wife'd be so fretted and outdone with him that she'd say that if a person went into a trance, they might as well stay in it, for Job hadn't been any use to the world since he come out of his.

"Well, when the revival was over, and all the converts had been received into the church, Brother Wilson called a meetin' o' the session and says he, 'There's two things to be done now. We've got to come up out of that old graveyard, and build a church in town that'll stand as a monument to this generation of Presbyterians long after their bodies have gone back to the old graveyard and moldered into dust; and while we're doing that,' says he, 'we must bring this congregation up to the standards the church has set for its members.' And he got the session to pass resolutions sayin' that all sinful and worldly pleasures like cyard-playin' and horse-racin' and dancin' was forbidden to church-members, and that the Sabbath day must be kept holy and no member of the church could ride or walk or take a journey on the Sabbath unless it was to do some work of necessity or mercy. Says he, 'This flock has been without a shepherd so long that the Good Shepherd himself could hardly tell which are the sheep and which are the goats. But,' says he, 'the time has come when every man has got to take his stand on the

HOUSE THAT WAS A WEDDING FEE

right hand or on the left, so the world can know what he is.'

"Well, of course these strict rulin's went mighty hard with some o' the church people, for, havin' been without a preacher so long, they'd got clean out of their religious ways. I ricollect they elected old Mr. Joe Bigsby superintendent of the Sunday-school, and the very first Sunday he was examinin' the children to see if their parents had taught 'em the things they ought to know, and he called on Johnny West to say the Lord's Prayer, and John was talkin' to the boy next to him and didn't hear. The old man was mighty quick-tempered, and he hollered out: 'John West! You John! Confound you, sir! Stand up and say the Lord's Prayer.' And then he ricollected himself, and he turned around to Brother Wilson, and says he, 'Now, I know that ain't any way for a Sunday-school superintendent to talk, but,' says he, 'jest give me a little time, and I'll git the hang o' this superintendent business.' Says he, 'When a Presbyterian's been without a church of his own for three years and been driftin' around loose amongst the Methodists and the Babtists, you've got to make some allowance for him.'

"Well, after he'd got the Sunday-school and the

THE LAND OF LONG AGO

weekly prayer-meetin' started, and all the church-members comin' regular to preachin', and everything runnin' smooth, Brother Wilson set about havin' the church built.

"The way they build churches now, child, is mighty different from the way they used to build 'em. Now nobody gives anything but money. It's money, money, money, every which way you turn. But in the olden time the way they built a church was like the way the Israelites built the tabernacle. You ricollect the Bible says, 'Every one whose heart stirred him up, and every one whom his spirit made willing, brought an offering to the Lord.' The rich men brought gold and silver, and the rulers brought onyx stones and oil and incense, and the poor men brought wood for the tabernacle and goats' skins and rams' skins, and the women they spun and wove and made purple and scyarlet cloth and fine linen. There wasn't anybody so poor that he couldn't give somethin' if his heart and his spirit was willin'. And that's the way it was when that Presbyterian church was built in the old time.

"The folks that was called rich then would be called poor nowadays, and a man's riches wasn't always money. But if one man had a sand-bank, he'd give sand

HOUSE THAT WAS A WEDDING FEE

for the mortar, and if another had good clay for makin' bricks, he'd give the clay, and somebody else that owned slaves'd give the labor — so many days' work — and there'd be the bricks for the walls; and if a church-member was a cyarpenter, he'd give so much of his time and his work, jest like the 'wise-hearted men' that worked on the tabernacle and made the curtains and the cherubims and the sockets of silver and brass and all the rest of the things that Moses commanded 'em to make.

"I reckon that old subscription paper'd look mighty strange nowadays. I ricollect one of the members said he'd give fifty dollars in cotton yarn at the price it was sellin' at in the stores; another said he'd give a hundred acres o' land in Monroe County; and another one give a hundred acres o' land 'way up in Illinois. One o' the elders said he'd give twenty-five dollars in shingles, and when he'd gethered his corn the next fall, he promised to give twenty-five barrels o' corn; another elder paid fifteen dollars in pork, and one o' the deacons who had a two-horse wagon paid sixty dollars in haulin'; and the saddlers and the tailors paid their part in saddlery and tailorin'. It's many a day, honey, since they laid the corner-stone o' that church, and there ain't a crack in the walls yet. The only good work is the work that love does, and in them days folks loved their churches jest as they loved their homes, and the work that went into that church was good work. I ricollect the Sunday they dedicated it the first hymn was,

> "'I love thy kingdom, Lord,
> The house of thine abode,
> The church our blest Redeemer saved
> With his own precious blood.'

"Me and Abram was there, for the country churches and the town churches was friendlier then than they are now. If the Goshen church was without a preacher Brother Wilson'd come out every third Sunday and preach for us, and if the weather and the travelin' was good, the Goshen folks'd go to town to preachin'.

"Now here I am tellin' about the dedicatin' of the church before I git through with the buildin'.

"Well, when the church was about half done, things begun to go wrong amongst the congregation. Somebody give a dancin'-party at the tavern, and two o' Judge Grace's daughters was there, and the old judge himself dropped in and looked at the dancin' a while; and before folks'd got through talkin' about that, here come the news that Squire Schuyler had taken a journey

HOUSE THAT WAS A WEDDING FEE

on the Sabbath day, and, besides that, he'd been heard usin' profane language. Of course it all come to Brother Wilson's ears, and as soon as he heard it he didn't lose any time callin' a meetin' of the session, and they summoned the old judge and the squire to appear before 'em and answer to the charges that was brought against 'em.

"The session was in the habit o' meetin' in old Doctor Brigham's office, and when they come together Judge Grace was on hand, and he explained how he'd gone to the tavern to bring his daughters home, and the gyirls wasn't quite ready to go home, and he had to stay and wait for 'em; and says he, 'I acknowledge that I did go into the hall where the young folks was dancin', and I stood and looked at 'em a while. And,' says he, 'I might 'a' patted my foot, keepin' time to the music, for they was dancin' a Virginia reel, and it's mighty hard for me to keep my feet still when there's a Virginia reel goin' on. But,' says he, 'that was the head and front of my offendin'.'

"Then Brother Wilson asked him if his daughters danced at the party, and the old judge he looked over at one o' the elders and winked, and then he says, as solemn as you please, 'Not while I was there.' Says he, 'I forbid my children to dance, and if I had known the nature of that party I would 'a' forbidden 'em to go to it. But,' says he, 'I can't say that my forbiddin' 'em would 'a' kept 'em from goin', but not bein' church-members,' says he, ' my daughters can't be disciplined for dancin', and if you're going to discipline the parents for what the children do,' says he, 'there's some ministers that'll have to be summoned to appear before the session.'

"And with that everybody laughed, and Brother Wilson he j'ined in as hearty as anybody, for he liked a joke, even when it was on himself. And says he, 'Well, that's one case settled.' And then he looks around, and says he, 'It seems that Squire Schuyler has not received the message from the session. Let the clerk of the session send him another summons, and to make sure of its reaching him, let one of the session hand it to him next Monday; that's county-court day, and he's certain to be in town.' So they fixed up another summons, and Judge Grace was to hand it to him.

"Well, when Monday mornin' come, the old judge took his stand on the corner o' the street in front o' the church and watched for the squire, and pretty soon

HOUSE THAT WAS A WEDDING FEE

here he come on horseback, gallopin' as hard as he could, and five or six hounds lopin' at the horse's heels.

"Squire Schuyler, honey, was a man different from any you see nowadays. As I look back on it now, it appears to me that he was the kind o' man that believed in gittin' all the pleasure he could out o' life. Nowadays everybody's tryin' so hard to make money, that they don't have time to enjoy life, and some of 'em wouldn't know how to enjoy it if they had the time. But Squire Schuyler was the kind that knows how to make the most out of everything that comes their way. The Schuyler family was a big family in Virginia 'way back in the time o' the first settlements. They had grants of land and lived high, and the two brothers that come to Kentucky had the same way of livin' and takin' things easy and makin' pleasure out o' life as they went along. Plenty o' money, plenty o' land, plenty o' slaves, fine horses, fine cattle, and a pack o' hounds — that's the way things was with the Schuylers, Meredith and Hamilton both. I can see Squire Meredith Schuyler now, the way he looked in that long overcoat made out o' dark green broadcloth with big brass buttons on it, ruffled shirt-bosom, high boots comin' 'way up to his knees, a broad-brimmed hat set back on his head

THE LAND OF LONG AGO

and a ridin'-whip in his hand, and long leather gloves, and the hounds skulkin' along behind him.

"That's the way he looked when Judge Grace walked up to him and handed him the second summons. And he opened the paper and read it, and then he tore it in two and threw it on the ground. And says he, 'Does the Rev. Samuel Wilson think that he's the Pope of Rome?' Says he, 'You go to him and tell him for me that this is a free country and I'm a free member of the Presbyterian church, and the journeys I take and the language I use are a matter between me and my conscience and my God.' And with that he walked off and left Judge Grace standin' there. And the judge he picked up the pieces o' paper and went right straight to Brother Wilson's house and told him what had happened. And Brother Wilson he listened to it all, and he looked mighty stern and says he, 'Call the session together at three o'clock this evening.' Says he, 'This is something that concerns the honor of the church, and we can't let the sun go down on it.'

"Well, the session, they all got together at the app'inted time, and Brother Wilson says, says he, 'Brethren, there's a serious question to be settled, and before we begin let us ask for light and wisdom

HOUSE THAT WAS A WEDDING FEE

from on high.' And then he prayed a prayer askin' the Lord to guide them in all they said and did, and when that was over, he called on Judge Grace to tell the session jest how Squire Schuyler had acted and talked when he handed him the summons. And the judge told it all jest so. 'And now,' says Brother Wilson, 'I want you gentlemen to understand that what Squire Schuyler said and did is not an insult to me.' Says he, 'I am not summoning him to come before this session.' Says he, 'The Squire has broken the rules of the church, and when he refuses to appear before the session, he's resisting the authority of the church, and when a man does that, why, there's nothing,' says he, 'for the church to do but to cut him off from its membership.'

"Well, the session, they looked at each other, and they hemmed and hawed, and finally Doctor Brigham says, says he, 'Brother Wilson, I believe you are right about this thing; but,' says he, 'it looks like this might be a case that calls for a little of the wisdom of the serpent.' Says he, 'You know there's good Scriptural authority for bein' "wise as serpents."' Says he, 'I know the Lord is no respecter of persons; but,' says he, 'there's times when common sense tells us to stop and consider a man's standin' and influence. Here we are,' says he, ' in the midst of buildin' a church. There's none too much money comin' to us, and Squire Schuyler's subscription is two or three times as big as anybody's, and, besides, it's all in hard money, and if we turn him out o' the church, we'll run short o' funds and have to stop buildin'.' Says he, ' If it was any time but now, I'd say, " Go ahead, and we'll all stand by you," but as we're buildin' a church, why, it looks to me like the wrong time to turn people out o' the church.'

"And Brother Wilson jumped up and says he, ' That's exactly the point I'm aiming at. We're building a church, and that is the reason why I want Squire Schuyler, and all members like him, deprived of church privileges.' Says he, ' What is a church, anyway? Is it that pile of brick and mortar you're putting up out yonder?' Says he, ' That's the church building, but the church itself,' says he, ' no eye but the eye of God has ever seen it, for it is builded of the hearts and consciences of men and women that have known the power of the spirit. That's the real church,' says he, ' and if you've got that, it matters not whether you've got the house of brick and stone or not.' Says he, ' When the Pilgrim Fathers set foot on Plymouth

HOUSE THAT WAS A WEDDING FEE

Rock and sang a hymn and knelt down and prayed under the open sky, *there* was a living church of the living God, and not a hypocrite or a mammon-worshiper or a time-server in it.' Says he, ' You men are mighty particular about the house for the church to worship in. You are looking for the best stone, and the best brick, and the best mortar; but when it comes to the building of the church itself, you're ready to put in hay, straw, and stubble for the sake of a little filthy lucre.'

" And all the time Brother Wilson was talkin', he was poundin' the table with his fist till the pens and the papers that was on it jest danced around, and Judge Grace said afterwards that he believed Brother Wilson'd rather have hit some o' the session than that table.

" Well, he sort o' stopped to take his breath, and Doctor Brigham says, says he, ' I agree with you, Brother Wilson, with all my heart. But there's another thing to be thought of before we do anything rash,' says he. ' Squire Schuyler ain't only a big contributor to the buildin' of the church, but he's the mainstay of the church when it comes to raisin' the preacher's salary. You've got a family dependin' on you.' says he, 'and do you think you'd be doin' justice to them to take a step that would cut your salary down?'

"I reckon the old doctor thought he'd pacify Brother Wilson and bring him to his senses, but instead o' pacifyin' him, it made him madder. He doubled up his fist and brought it down on the table again, and says he, 'If a minister of the gospel has to neglect his duty in order to earn his salary and support his family, then it's time for honest men to get out of the pulpit and make room for scoundrels that'll sell their principles and their self-respect for a matter of a few dollars and cents.' Says he, 'No matter how poor I am, I've never been so poor that I couldn't afford to do right. I left the army for the church, and I can go from the church back to the army; for,' says he, 'I'd rather be a ragged, barefooted soldier in the ranks, living on half rations and fighting in a good cause, than a cowardly, skulking preacher dressed in broadcloth and sitting down on his conscience every time he opened his mouth.' And with that he took up his hat and went out o' the office, slammin' the door after him.

"And Judge Grace says to Doctor Brigham, 'Where do you reckon that preacher of ours got his notions of what's right and what's wrong?' And Doctor

HOUSE THAT WAS A WEDDING FEE

Brigham shook his head and says he, 'I reckon he got 'em from the Bible, for,' says he, 'such notions and such conduct might do in the days when preachers was fed by the ravens, but they don't fit into this day and generation when a preacher has to preach for his livin'.'

"Well, town news can travel to the country as fast as country news can travel to town, and of course Squire Schuyler wasn't long hearin' about the meetin' of the session, and as soon as he heard it he got on his horse and rode to town, and went right straight to Doctor Brigham's office — the doctor was the treasurer of the church — and says he, 'I understand that you gentlemen of the session are considering the question of turning me out of the church, and some of you think my subscription won't be paid if that's done. I want you to understand,' says he, 'that my word is better than any man's bond. I promised to give a thousand dollars toward the church buildin'; here's a check for fifteen hundred. Now turn me out if you want to. You've got nothing to lose by turning me out and nothing to gain by keeping me in.'

"That ain't exactly what Meredith Schuyler said, honey," remarked Aunt Jane, pausing in her story to make an explanatory note. "Jest exactly what he

THE LAND OF LONG AGO

said it wouldn't be right for me or any Christian woman to tell, for Meredith Schuyler never opened his mouth, unless it was to eat his meals, that he didn't take the name o' the Lord in vain. But that was the sum and substance of it.

"Well, Doctor Brigham he went straight to Brother Wilson's house and showed him the check, and told him about meetin' the squire and all that had passed between 'em, and Brother Wilson he slapped his knee, and says he, 'Now we'll have a meeting of the session to-morrow and settle the matter right away.' So they all met again in the doctor's office, and Brother Wilson called the meetin' to order and says he, 'I have been asking the Lord to turn the hearts and minds of my session that they might see certain matters as I see them. I cannot tell whether my prayer has been answered,' says he, 'but the thing that kept some of you from doing your duty last week has been providentially removed, and the way is clear before our feet. Squire Schuyler,' says he, 'has not only paid his subscription, but he has paid five hundred dollars more than his subscription. I move that Judge Grace be a committee of one to write the squire a letter accepting his gift, and thanking him for his liberality.'

HOUSE THAT WAS A WEDDING FEE

"Well, they seconded the motion, and Judge Grace said he'd be glad to write the letter, and then Brother Wilson says, 'The payment of that money shows that Squire Schuyler is an open-hearted, open-handed gentleman. I wish I could say Christian gentleman,' says he, 'but the charges of profanity and Sabbath-breaking are still standing against him, and we must now do our duty and deprive him of the rights and privileges of church-membership.'

"Well, they said Doctor Brigham and Judge Grace both threw up their hands and begun talkin' at once, and says they, 'You don't mean to say you're goin' to turn the squire out now!' And Brother Wilson says, says he, 'Why not? Here are the charges against him: breaking the Sabbath, taking the name of the Lord in vain, and refusing to appear before the officers of the church when he's summoned.' And Doctor Brigham says, 'But he's paid his subscription.' And Brother Wilson says, 'That's no more than an honest man ought to do.' And Judge Grace says, 'But he's paid five hundred dollars besides.' And Brother Wilson says, 'A letter of thanks is all we owe him for that.' Says he, 'Here's a matter of church discipline, and here's a matter of money, and one has nothing whatever

THE LAND OF LONG AGO

to do with the other. Can't you see that?' says he. And they all shook their heads and said they couldn't. And Judge Grace says: 'It looks to me like it's not treatin' a man exactly square to take his money to build the church, and then to turn him out o' the church. It looks like if a man's money's good enough to go into the church walls, the man's name's good enough to stay on the church rolls.' And the rest of the session, they agreed with the old judge. But Brother Wilson, he jumped up and says he, 'A man that sees things that way has a conscience that needs enlightening.' Says he, 'Money itself is neither good nor evil. Whether it's clean or unclean,' says he, 'depends on the way it's given and the way it's taken. The money that's given in fulfilment of a promise,' says he, 'is clean money: let it go into the walls of the church. Coming from Meredith Schuyler's hands the way it does,' says he, 'it's pure gold. He's not offering it as a bribe to us to keep him in the church, but if we take it as a bribe,' says he, 'the minute it gets into our hands it turns to base coin, and it's a dishonor to us who take it and an insult to him who gave it.'

"Well, the session set there and studied a while, and shook their heads, and said they couldn't see things

HOUSE THAT WAS A WEDDING FEE

that way. And Brother Wilson looked at 'em a minute or two, and then he jumped up and says he, 'Let us pray.' And then he offered up a prayer that God would send his spirit into the hearts and consciences of his servants, that they might see things in the right light, so that all they did might be for the glory of God and of his kingdom on earth. Then they all set down and waited a while, and Brother Wilson says, 'Brethren, are you still of the same mind?' And they all nodded their heads, and says he, 'Well, when the session thinks one way and the minister another, it's time for them to separate.' Says he, 'Here's my resignation by word of mouth, and as soon as I go home, I'll put it in writing.' And off he went, leavin' the session sittin' there.

"Well, of course the men went home and told their wives all about it, and before the next day everybody was talkin' about Brother Wilson resignin', and the church-members lined up, some on the squire's side and some on the preacher's side, jest like they did in Goshen church the time we got the new organ. There was the church walls goin' up, and both sides had put money into 'em, and neither side had money enough to buy the other side out, and neither side wanted to be

THE LAND OF LONG AGO

bought out. And the squire's side, they'd say, 'We've got the money, and you can't have a church without money.' And the preacher's side, they'd say, 'But we've got the members and the preacher, and you can't have a church without church-members and a preacher.' And they had it up and down and back and forth, and the Methodists and Babtists, they took sides, and such quarrelin' and disputin' you never heard. Some o' the outsiders went to Brother Wilson, and says they, 'You Christian people are settin' a mighty bad example to us outsiders. Can't somethin' be done,' says they, 'to stop this wranglin' amongst the churches?'

"And Brother Wilson, he laughed at 'em, and says he, 'Open your Bibles and find out who it was said, "I came not to send peace, but a sword."' Says he, 'The word of the Lord is a two-edged sword, and all this disturbance means that the Lord is visiting his church and his spirit is striving with the spirit of man.'

"Well, matters was standin' in this loose, unj'inted way when all at once Squire Schuyler's weddin' invitations come out. Everybody knew he was waitin' on Miss Drusilla Elrod, but nobody expected the weddin' that soon, and folks begun speculatin' about who he'd have say the weddin' ceremony, and Judge Grace

HOUSE THAT WAS A WEDDING FEE

says: 'Now see what a man makes by havin' such curious ideas and bein' so rash in his speech. Here's a big weddin' fee that ought to go into a Presbyterian pocket, and instead o' that, it'll fall to some Babtist or Methodist preacher.'

"But — bless your life! — the day before the weddin', Squire Schuyler's carriage drove up to the parsonage, and the coachman got out and knocked at the door and handed in a letter with a big red seal, and it was from the squire, askin' Brother Wilson to say the weddin' ceremony over him, and promisin' to send his carriage to bring him and Mis' Wilson to the weddin'.

"Well, that weddin' was the talk o' the town and the country for many a day before and after it happened. They had cyarpet spread from the gate to the front door, and they burned over a hundred wax candles before the evenin' was over, and folks said it looked like they had ransacked the heavens above and the earth beneath and the waters under the earth for somethin' to put on that supper-table. Brother Wilson said a mighty nice ceremony over 'em, and when they went out to supper the preacher and his wife set on the right hand of the bride and groom.

"Well, when Brother Wilson got ready to leave,

THE LAND OF LONG AGO

he went up to Squire Schuyler to shake hands and say good night, and the squire pulled a long paper out o' the breast pocket of his coat, and he bowed, and says he, 'Will you do me the honor, sir, to accept this?' Squire Schuyler had a mighty grand way of talkin', honey, and you don't see any such manners nowadays as the Schuylers and the Elrods used to have. And says he, 'Don't open it till you get home.' And Brother Wilson, he says, 'I'm not the man to look a gift horse in the mouth, but,' says he, 'I must see the gift horse before I accept it.' With that he opened the paper, and what do you reckon it was, honey? It was a deed to that house I p'inted out to you the day we went to town — Schuyler Hall, they call it — and I don't know how many acres of land along with it.

"Brother Wilson he looked at it and looked at it, and it seemed as if he couldn't take it in. And says he, 'There must be some mistake about this. You surely do not mean to deed me a house and land?'

"And the squire he bows again, and says he, 'There's no mistake. The house and the land are yours to have and to hold while you live and to will as you please when you die.'

"And Brother Wilson held out the paper and says he,

HOUSE THAT WAS A WEDDING FEE

'Sir, it's a princely gift, but I can't take it. It's no suitable fee for a poor preacher like myself.'

" And the squire he folded his arms and stepped back to keep Brother Wilson from puttin' the deed into his hands, and says he, ' It takes a princely gift to suit an occasion like this.' Says he, ' I want the wedding fee to match the worth of my bride and the worth of my minister, but, not being a prince, this is the best I can do.' And all the time he was talkin', Brother Wilson was shakin' his head and tryin' to make him take back the paper, and sayin', ' I can't take it, I can't take it.'

" And the squire says: ' Sir, you'll have to take it. The deed has passed from my hands to yours, and a Schuyler never takes back a gift.' And Brother Wilson, he says, ' But the gift will be of no use to me. I've handed in my resignation,' says he, ' and the presbytery will shortly send me to another field of usefulness.'

" And the squire he ripped out a terrible oath, and says he, ' I beg your pardon, sir, for swearing in your presence. I've heard,' says he, ' of the doings of that session; but,' says he, ' if I have influence enough to keep myself in the church, I have influence enough to keep you in, too; and if I can't do that,' says he,

THE LAND OF LONG AGO

'I'll build you a church and pay you a salary for life.' Says he, 'There's nothing too good for a man that refuses to bow down and worship the golden calf.'

"Honey," said Aunt Jane, lowering her voice, "considerin' it was his weddin' night and him talkin' to a preacher, the language Squire Schuyler used was far from fittin'. What he said was all right, but the way he said it was all wrong.

"Well, they argued back and forth, and it ended by Brother Wilson goin' home with the deed in his pocket. And the next Saturday Squire Schuyler come before the session and acknowledged the error of his ways. 'And,' says he, 'I promise in future to keep the Sabbath day holy, but as to the profane language,' says he, 'it comes as natural to me to swear and fight as it does to the Rev. Mr. Wilson to pray and fight, and all I can promise about that,' says he, 'is that hereafter I'll try to do the most of my swearing in private, so my example won't hurt the church I'm a member of.'

"And Sunday mornin', child, here come Squire Schuyler and his bride, as fine as a fiddle, walkin' down the church aisle arm in arm, and the squire j'ined in the hymns, and when the contribution plate was passed around he dropped a gold piece on it as unconcerned

HOUSE THAT WAS A WEDDING FEE

as if it was a copper cent. And Brother Wilson, he moved out to the house the squire had give him, and there never was anybody as happy as he appeared to be. He'd walk around under the trees and look at his gyarden on one side and his clover-fields on the other side, and he'd say: ' " Delight thyself in the Lord, and he shall give thee the desires of thine heart." I've always wanted a home in the country, and the Lord has given me one of the desires of my heart.'

" But he didn't live to enjoy it very long, poor man. He died before his prime, and his tombstone's standin' now in the old graveyard yonder in town. They had a Bible text cyarved on it, ' For he was a good man, and full of the Holy Ghost and of God, and much people was added unto the Lord.'

" And now, child, put on your hat. I see Johnny Amos comin' with the buggy, and we'll go over and see the old house."

Suppose a child should read the story of Beauty and the Beast, and straightway a fairy godmother should appear, saying, " Now, let us go to the palace of the Beast." If you can fancy that child's feelings, you will know how I felt when I stepped into the old buggy to go to Schuyler Hall.

THE LAND OF LONG AGO

It was a gray September afternoon. The air was warm and still, and the earth lay weary, thirsty, and patient under a three-weeks drouth. Dust was thick over the grass, flowers, and trees along the roadside, and on the weed-grown fields that had brought forth their harvest for the sons of men and now, sun-scorched and desolate, seemed to say, " Is this the end, the end of all ? "

Over the horizon there was a soft haze like smoke from the smoldering embers of summer's dying fires, and in the west gloomed a cloud from which the thunder and the lightning would be loosed before the midnight hour; and after the rain would come a season of gentle suns, cool dews, and frosts scarce colder than the dew — not spring, but a memory of spring — when the earth, looking back to her May, would send a ripple of green over the autumn fields, and, like thoughts of youth in the heart of age, the clover and the dandelion would spring into untimely bloom.

" Things look sort o' down-hearted and discouraged, don't they ? " said Aunt Jane, echoing my thought. " But jest wait till the Lord sends us the latter rain, and things'll freshen up mightily. There's plenty o' pretty weather to come betwixt now and winter-time.

HOUSE THAT WAS A WEDDING FEE

Now, child, you jump out and open the gate, like I used to do in the days when I was young and spry."

Old Nelly crept lazily up the long avenue, and my eyes were fixed on the house of legend that lay at its end.

"Houses and lands are jest like pieces o' money," observed Aunt Jane. "They pass from one hand to another, and this old place has had many an owner since Brother Wilson's day. The man that owns it now is a great-nephew of old Peter Cyartwright, and him and his wife's mighty proud of the place."

"Do they object to strangers coming to see it?" I asked as we neared the giant cypress-tree in front of the porch.

"La, child," laughed Aunt Jane. "Ain't this Kentucky? Who ever heard of a Kentuckian objectin' to folks goin' through his house! We'll jest walk in at the front door and out at the back door and see all that's to be seen, up-stairs and down."

As she spoke we heard the voice of the hostess bidding us welcome to Schuyler Hall, and, fresh from the fairy-land of Aunt Jane's memories, I walked into one of the scenes of the story, the house that was a wedding fee.

THE LAND OF LONG AGO

There was a hint of baronial grandeur in the lofty ceilings, the heavy walnut wainscoting and oaken floors, the huge fireplaces with their tall mantels; and underneath the evident remodeling and repairing one saw the home and the taste of a vanished generation, the same that had witnessed the building of Monticello, for the hand that wrote the Declaration of Independence had drawn the plans for the house that was a wedding fee.

From room to room I went, pleasing myself with fancies of the man who had never bowed the knee to Mammon. My feet were on the floors that he had trod. By this worn hearthstone he had knelt, night and morn, to the God who had given him the desire of his heart. From this doorway he had looked upon the broad acres that were his by grace of a generous adversary, the tribute of one noble nature to another. In the long, low-ceiled bedchamber above the stately lower rooms he had slept the sleep of one whose conscience is void of offense toward God and his fellow man, and through the dormer-window that looked toward the rising of the sun his soul had passed out in its flight to the stars.

Dusty and flowerless, the garden paths wandered to

HOUSE THAT WAS A WEDDING FEE

right and left, but not one did I miss in my pilgrimage; for who could know what shrines of remembrance might lie hidden in that drift of leaves, withered and fallen before their time? Perhaps the minister's hand had planted the clump of tansy and the bed of sage, and well I knew that here in the night hours he had met his Maker, and his garden had been to him as that paradise where Adam walked with God.

Near the house was a spring to whose waters came the Indian and the deer before the foot of the pioneer had touched Kentucky soil. Rising from sources too deep to be affected by the weather of earth, no drouth ever checks its flow, no flood increases it, and here I knelt and drank to the memory of a day that is not dead nor can ever die.

Again on the threshold of the old house I paused and looked back into the shadowy hall. Ah, if the other world would for a moment give up its own that I might see them " in their habit as they lived," the Cavalier squire, the Puritan minister, the bride whose womanly worth was but faintly shadowed forth in the princely gift of a house and land! But no presence crossed the dim perspective within, and the only whisper I heard was the wind in the cypress-tree. The past had buried its dead, and soon their habitation, like themselves, would be but a memory and a name.

> In that mansion used to be
> Free-hearted hospitality;
> His great fires up the chimney roared,
> The stranger feasted at his board.

Fair and stately are the dwellings that shelter this latest generation, and by their side such mansions as Schuyler Hall seem only moldering, ghost-haunted reminders of the past. But those who dwelt in them are immortal, and though walls of flesh and walls of stone alike crumble to dust, there shall never lack a heart to treasure and a pen to record the virtues of the men and women of those early times, who, in reverence and in honor, founded and built the " old Kentucky home."

III
THE COURTSHIP OF MISS AMARYLLIS

III

THE COURTSHIP OF MISS AMARYLLIS

"IT'S curious," said Aunt Jane meditatively, "how, when old people go to lookin' back on the way things was when they was young, it appears like everything was better then than it is now. Strawberries was sweeter, times was easier, men was taller, and women prettier. I ain't sayin' a word against your looks, child; you're as good-lookin' as the best of 'em

THE LAND OF LONG AGO

nowadays, but I reckon there ain't any harm in me sayin' that you don't quite come up to Miss Penelope and Miss Amaryllis. I git to thinkin' about them two, and I wish I could see 'em by the side o' the women that folks call pretty nowadays so I could tell whether they really was prettier or whether it's jest an old woman's notion."

"Who was Miss Amaryllis?" I asked. "If she matched her name she must have been a beauty."

Aunt Jane smiled delightedly and gave an assenting nod. "Miss Amaryllis was Miss Penelope's sister," she said. "They was first cousins to Dick Elrod, that married Annie Crawford, and their father was Judge Elrod, Squire Elrod's brother. The old judge was a mighty learned sort of a man. He spent most of his time readin' and writin', and he had a room in his house with nothin' in it but books, clear from the floor to the ceilin', and some of 'em he never allowed anybody but himself to touch, he thought so much of 'em. And next to his books it was his two daughters. Folks used to say that the judge's wife was right jealous of his books and of Miss Penelope and Miss Amaryllis.

"Maybe you know, child, where the old judge got the names for his daughters. The only names I'm

COURTSHIP OF MISS AMARYLLIS

used to are the good old family names that come out o' the Bible, and some people said Penelope and Amaryllis couldn't be called Christian names, because they sounded so heathenish, and the judge's wife she objected to 'em because, she said, they was too long for folks to say. But the old judge wouldn't hear to anybody's shortenin' the children's names. Says he, 'If you give a child a plain name it'll be likely to turn out a plain man or a plain woman. But,' says he, 'I've given my children fine names, and I expect them to grow up into women that'll become their names.' And I reckon they did, for two prettier women you never saw, and their names seemed to suit 'em exactly. And as for their bein' too long, I always liked to say 'em and hear people say 'em. Penelope and Amaryllis — why, they're jest as easy to say as Mary and Marthy, and I always thought they sounded like fallin' water or the singin' of a bird, Amaryllis especially."

Aunt Jane paused here and laid down her work. She had reached a difficult point in the story, and there must be time for thought.

"Now, how in the world am I goin' to tell you how Miss Amaryllis looked?" she said, with an accent of gentle despair. "Why, it's as hard as tryin' to tell about

THE LAND OF LONG AGO

that yeller rose that grew in old lady Elrod's gyarden. There never was such a rose as that, and there never was such a gyirl as Miss Amaryllis, or Miss Penelope either, for that matter. The judge was always havin' their pictures painted, and there was one, no bigger around than that, set in gold. If I jest had it to show you! But I reckon that picture o' Miss Amaryllis is lyin' in a grave somewhere on the other side o' the ocean. Mighty near every woman has somethin' pretty about her; one'll have pretty eyes and another 'll have a pretty color, but Miss Amaryllis was pretty every way. I ricollect once I was passin' along Main Street, one County Court day, and the old judge's carriage was standin' in front o' Tom Barker's dry-goods store, and Miss Amaryllis was leanin' back against the cushions, and her hand was layin' on the carriage door, and she had a ring on one of her fingers with a yeller stone in it; the sun was shinin' on it and, I declare to goodness, from that day to this I never see a white lily with the yeller heart and the dust like grains o' gold inside of it that I don't think o' Miss Amaryllis's hand and Miss Amaryllis's ring.

"They both had golden hair, Miss Penelope and Miss Amaryllis, but Miss Penelope had gray eyes

MISS PENELOPE AND MISS AMARYLLIS.
Page 80.

COURTSHIP OF MISS AMARYLLIS

like a dove's, and Miss Amaryllis had brown ones with dark lashes. I reckon it was Miss Amaryllis's eyes and hair that made her what she was. You can find plenty o' women with brown eyes and brown hair, but when you find one with brown eyes and golden hair, why, it's somethin' to ricollect. And then, there was her voice. You've heard me tell many a time about Miss Penelope's voice, and Miss Amaryllis had one that was jest as sweet, but hers was low and deep where Miss Penelope's was clear and high. Miss Amaryllis played on the guitar, and summer nights they'd sit out on the portico and sing together, and the old judge used to say that when his gyirls sung the very mockin'-birds stopped to listen.

"Many a woman has hard work to find one man to love her, and many a woman can't find even one, but Miss Amaryllis had more beaus on her string, and more strings to her bow, than any fiddler in the state; and she danced with 'em and sung to 'em and played with 'em like a cat plays with mice, and then, when she got ready, she'd send 'em on their way, and she'd go on hers. And as fast as one went another'd come. The judge's wife used to shake her head and say,

THE LAND OF LONG AGO

'My daughter, there's such a thing as a woman sayin' "No" once too often.' And Miss Amaryllis she'd say, 'Yes, and there's such a thing as a woman sayin' "Yes" a little too soon;' and the old judge he'd laugh and say, 'Let her alone; one of these days she'll find her master.' And sure enough she did. They said it was love at first sight on both sides when Miss Amaryllis and Hamilton Schuyler met each other at a big party at Squire Elrod's, and before long the weddin' day was set, and everybody was sayin' that Miss Amaryllis had found her match at last.

"Hamilton Schuyler was as handsome as Miss Amaryllis was pretty, and when it come to family he had as much to brag of as she had. He was a first cousin to Squire Meredith Schuyler, and all the Schuylers had fine houses and plenty o' land. Rich folks in that day had a way of namin' their places jest as rich folks do now. The Elrod place was called The Cedars, and Hamilton Schuyler had a big house on the same 'pike, and that was Schuyler Court. The Schuylers was mighty proud o' their blood, and I used to hear folks talk about the coat of arms that the squire had hangin' in his front hall. Abram was there once to see about some land the squire was havin' cleared, and he said

COURTSHIP OF MISS AMARYLLIS

he took particular notice of the coat of arms, but to save his life he couldn't see why they called it that, for there wasn't any coat or any arms on it that he could see, jest a curious colored thing, red and blue and black, and on top of it some kind of a beast standin' on its hind legs.

"The Elrods come of plain people at the start, but they could hold up their heads with the best, for they had plenty o' money and plenty o' learnin', too, and the judge's wife was as blue-blooded as any Schuyler and twice as proud of her blood, in the bargain. She had pictures, and silver things, and dishes that'd been in the family for generations, and her great-great-grandfather was a Fairfax.

"There's some people, child, that'll tell you that one person's as good as another, and all blood's alike, and all of it red. And maybe they are right. And when it comes to kindness and right principles and all that, why, Squire Schuyler and the judge's wife wasn't a bit better'n Abram and me. But when it come to their manners and their language, they had somethin' we didn't have. Abram was jest as polite a man as Squire Schuyler, but he couldn't take off his hat to a lady the way the squire could, and I couldn't bow and smile like the judge's wife, and I reckon that's where the blue blood comes in.

"I ricollect talkin' to Parson Page once about this very thing, and he says, 'The Lord hath made of one blood all the nations of the earth, and in His sight there is neither high nor low according to blood.' Says he, 'The Lord looks at the life and the conscience of a man to tell whether he's high or low; and,' says he, 'in His sight there's little difference between the good man who is born in the high places of the earth and the good man who walks in lowly paths. Both are pure gold, but one's been shaped and stamped by goin' through the mint, and the other's rough in the nugget.'

"Now, what was I startin' out to tell you, child, before I got to talkin' about blue blood? Oh, yes, I ricollect now.

"Well, everybody was lookin' for Miss Amaryllis's weddin' cyards, when, all at once, her and Hamilton had a quarrel, and the match was broke off then and there. It was a long time before anybody knew what had happened betwixt the two, but at last it come out that they'd quarreled about where they'd live after they married. Of course he expected to take his bride to his own house, and of course any right-minded woman would 'a' been willin' to go with her husband; but when he happened to say somethin' about the time when she'd be livin' at Schuyler Court, she give him to understand that she couldn't leave The Cedars, and that whoever married her would have to live at her father's house.

"Now it's my belief, honey, that Miss Amaryllis hadn't any idea of makin' Hamilton Schuyler leave Schuyler Court and come and live at The Cedars. She was jest foolin' when she said that. She'd been used to twistin' the men round her little finger all her life, and she wanted to see if Hamilton was like all the rest. But Hamilton took it all in earnest, and he said whoever heard of a man givin' up his own home and goin' to live with his father-in-law, and did she want him to be the laughin'-stock of the whole country? And she said that if he cared more for his house than he cared for her he could stay at Schuyler Court and she'd stay at The Cedars. And he said it wasn't Schuyler Court he cared for; he'd leave Schuyler Court and build her another house anywhere she wanted to live, but if she wouldn't leave her father's house, then he'd have to believe that she cared more for The Cedars than she cared for him. And they had it up and down and back and forth, and at last she give him back his ring and sent him away jest like she'd sent the others.

"The judge and his wife was terribly upset about it. They both loved Hamilton like he was their own son, and the old lady said that Miss Amaryllis had thrown away her best chance, and maybe her last one, and she grieved mightily, for in that day, honey, an old-maid daughter wasn't considered a blessin' by any means. They tried their best to git Hamilton and Miss Amaryllis to make up, but he said he was certain she didn't love him as well as a woman ought to love the man she was goin' to marry, and she said a man who wouldn't try to please a woman before marriage wouldn't be likely to try to please her after they married; and he said he'd be willin' to give up his way, if he was only certain she loved him right, and she said how could a woman love a man that put his pleasure before hers? And the longer the old people argued with her, the more contrairy it made Miss Amaryllis, and finally they had to give it up.

"Of course all her old beaus come flockin' back as soon as they heard that Miss Amaryllis had give Hamilton his walkin'-papers, and things was as gay as ever at The Cedars. But Hamilton, he settled down at

COURTSHIP OF MISS AMARYLLIS

Schuyler Court, and it looked like all the pleasure he had in life was gone. Some men, if they can't git the woman they want, they'll take one they don't want and manage to put up with her tolerable well. But Hamilton wasn't that sort. With him it was the woman he loved or nobody.

"Well, the judge dropped off right sudden with paralysis, and in a year or two the old lady followed him, and Miss Penelope married, and there was Miss Amaryllis all alone in the big house with jest the housekeeper, Miss Sempronia Davis, and the family servants; and there was Hamilton off yonder in Schuyler Court, pale and thin and quiet, and the years passin', and both of 'em lovin' each other more every day, and losin' their happiness and wastin' their lives all on account of a foolish little quarrel.

"They said the judge always felt hard towards Miss Amaryllis for disapp'intin him so, but he divided the property even betwixt her and Miss Penelope and give her The Cedars. 'I give and bequeath to my daughter Amaryllis The Cedars, since she seems to care more for this than for anything else in the world ' — that was the way the will was.

"I reckon most women would 'a' lost their beauty

livin' the way Miss Amaryllis did, everything goin' wrong with her, and old age certain to come, but it looked like all that time could do to her was to make her prettier, and there wasn't a young gyirl in the country that could hold a candle to her.

"I don't exactly ricollect how long things went on this way, but I reckon death would 'a' found 'em holdin' out against each other if Schuyler Court hadn't burned.

"They said Hamilton had been lookin' over old papers and letters durin' the day, and he'd thrown a lot of 'em into the fireplace and put a match to 'em, and the chimney bein' old and the mortar between the bricks crumbled away in places, some o' the sparks must 'a' got to the rafters, and before they found it out the roof was pretty near ready to fall. The slaves worked hard to save the furniture and things down-stairs, but they said Hamilton didn't seem to keer whether anything was saved or not. He'd lost the woman he loved, and the house was partly the cause of it; and so I reckon the loss of the house was a small matter. He jest stood with his arms folded and watched the walls crumble and fall, and then he walked over to the little cabin where the overseer had his office, and he set

COURTSHIP OF MISS AMARYLLIS

down and dropped his head in his hands and never stirred nor spoke all the rest of the night. And the next day he was still sittin' there when one of Miss Amaryllis's slaves come in and handed him a letter. He took it and read it, and they said he acted like somebody raised from the dead. He rushed to the stable and saddled his horse and got to The Cedars ahead of the slave that'd brought the letter, and when he got there every servant on the place was standin' at the gate bowin' and scrapin' and sayin': 'Howdy, mahster! Howdy, mahster!' and Miss Sempronia met him at the door and says she: 'Walk up-stairs, sir. Your room is ready. Miss Amaryllis herself fixed it for you.' And Hamilton followed her, not knowin' what it all meant, and expectin' every minute to see Miss Amaryllis; and when they got up-stairs Miss Sempronia showed him his room and handed him another letter, and then she went on down-stairs, leavin' him to read the letter.

"And what do you reckon Miss Amaryllis had done? Why, she'd given him The Cedars — the house and everything in it and all the slaves that belonged to the place. I reckon Hamilton was like Brother Wilson when he got his weddin' fee from the squire. He couldn't take it in at first, and when he begun to see what she'd done he run out o' the room and downstairs callin' her name: 'Amaryllis! Amaryllis!' And the housekeeper, she met him at the bottom o' the stairs, and says she, 'Miss Amaryllis is not here.' And says he, 'Not here? Then where is she?' And Miss Sempronia says, 'That's something that nobody knows. You know Miss Amaryllis is not in the habit of giving an account of herself to other people, and all I know is that she left The Cedars early this morning on horseback, but where she went I can't say, and as to her coming back,' says she, 'the place belongs to you now, and it wouldn't be proper for her to be here.'

"'Which way did she go?' says Hamilton. 'Tell me that.'

"'She went towards town,' says Miss Sempronia. And before the words was out of her mouth, Hamilton was out o' the front door and on his way to town. They said he stopped everybody he met on the road and asked if they'd seen Miss Amaryllis, and when he got to town, he found out that Miss Amaryllis had been seen gettin' into the stage and goin' in the direction of Bell's Tavern. So he set out for the tavern. I reckon you've heard o' Bell's Tavern, child. That

COURTSHIP OF MISS AMARYLLIS

was a great stoppin'-place in your grandfather's day. Folks was always sure of a good meal when they got to that tavern, and the drinks Uncle Billy mixed was famous all over the State.

"Well, Hamilton come gallopin' up to the gate and jumped off and threw his bridle to the boy that looked after the travelers' horses. He rushed into the tavern, and says he, 'I'm looking for Miss Amaryllis Elrod. Has she been this way?'

"Uncle Billy was sittin' in a big hickory chair with one of his feet all bandaged and propped up on another chair. The old man suffered a heap from rheumatism. He had a bottle and a tumbler and a bowl of honey on the table by him, and he was mixin' one of his peach-and-honey toddies — peach-brandy sweetened with honey instead of sugar. Well, he didn't even look up, bein' so used to people comin' in and goin' out. He jest went on stirrin' his toddy and puttin' in a little more honey and a little more peach. And at last he says, 'Yes, she's been this way.'

"And Hamilton says: 'Where is she? Where is she?' right quick and sharp. And Uncle Billy went on stirrin', and at last he says, 'I don't know.' And Hamilton says: 'Is she here? Has she gone? Which

THE LAND OF LONG AGO

way did she go?' And Uncle Billy says: 'Maybe it's my time to ask a few questions. What's your name, and who are you, anyway?' And Hamilton says, 'My name's Hamilton Schuyler, at your service, sir, if you'll tell me which way the lady went.'

"And with that Uncle Billy took a good look at him and says he, 'Why, Hamilton, is this you? I reckon that last toddy must 'a' gone to my eyes for me not to know you, when I knew your mother and your father before you.' Says he, 'You've been chasin' Miss Amaryllis for five years or more. How does it happen you haven't caught up with her yet? I beg your pardon for talkin' so short a while ago, but,' says he, 'when a man comes along askin' me which way a woman went, I've got to know somethin' about the man before I tell him what he wants to know.' Says he, 'Sit down and have a toddy with me.' And Hamilton, he thanked him and says he, 'No toddy for me, Uncle Billy. Tell me which way the lady went, and I'm off.'

"Uncle Billy he laughed and stirred his toddy, tryin' to make the honey and the brandy mix, and says he, 'That's the way with you young fellers. I've seen the day when a toddy couldn't 'a' stopped me from

COURTSHIP OF MISS AMARYLLIS

follerin' after a gyirl; but now,' says he, 'I'd hate to have to choose betwixt a woman and this here peach and honey.' And Hamilton, he was tappin' his boot with his ridin'-whip and walkin' the floor, and Uncle Billy jest kept on talkin' and stirrin'. 'You're young and strong,' says he, 'and I'm old and feeble. It's half-past ten in the mornin' with you, and it's half-past eleven at night with me. You're on the big road, and jest before you there's a gyirl with yeller hair and brown eyes, and you'll ketch up with her maybe before night, and here I am in my old hickory chair and nothin' before me but my old lame foot and my peach and honey. But,' says he, 'son, take an old man's advice: don't be in too big a hurry to ketch up with that yeller-haired gyirl.' Says he, 'You know the old sayin' about a bird in the hand bein' worth two in the bush, but from long experience,' says he, 'I've learned that it's the other way with women. A woman in the bush is worth two in the hand, so keep her in the bush as long as you can.'

"Well, they said Hamilton burst out laughin', and seein' that the old man was too far gone to give him any information, he called up all the servants on the place, and he pulled out a handful o' silver and threw it around amongst 'em, and by questionin' this one and that one he found out which way Miss Amaryllis had gone, and away he went after her as hard as he could gallop. And, to make a long story short, he hunted around over the biggest half of Warren County, and he wore out two or three horses, before he found Miss Amaryllis.

"She'd gone to a big country place where one of her cousins on the Elrod side lived, and when Hamilton got there early one mornin', he found there was goin' to be a party that night, and everybody for miles around was to be there. So he rode back to town and went to the county clerk's office and got his license, and then he found out where the Presbyterian minister lived, and he went there and told him who he was and what he'd come for. The minister he thought a minute and says he, 'I don't know what my congregation will say about me going to a dance to perform a wedding ceremony. Can't you wait till to-morrow morning?' They said Hamilton stamped his foot and swore — swearin' was a Schuyler failin' — and says he, 'I've waited five years, and here you ask me to wait till to-morrow morning.' Says he, 'Is there water or milk in your veins?'

COURTSHIP OF MISS AMARYLLIS

"And the minister laughed, and says he, 'No, there's blood in my veins, the same as there is in yours, and I'm a man before I'm a preacher. I'll go with you, dancing or no dancing, and see the thing through.' And Hamilton laughed, and says he, 'It's not a dance you're going to; it's a wedding.'

"Well, he and the young preacher set out for the country place where Miss Amaryllis was stayin', and got there jest as the fiddlers was tunin' up for the first dance and all the men was choosin' their partners. Hamilton had on his ridin'-clothes, but no matter what kind o' clothes he had on, he always had a grand sort of a look, and they said when he come into the big room, everybody turned around and stopped talkin'. And he stood still a minute, lookin' for Miss Amaryllis, and as soon as he saw her, he walked straight up and took hold of her hand, and says he, 'The next dance is mine.' And the young man that was standin' by Miss Amaryllis he fired up and says he, 'You're mistaken. Miss Amaryllis has promised me this dance.' And Hamilton, he bowed and says he, 'Five years ago, sir, she promised me the next dance, and I've been traveling night and day for a week to have that promise kept.' And he looks down at Miss Amaryllis and says he, 'Isn't that so?' And she smiles at the young man and nods her head, and jest then the music struck up and she danced off with Hamilton.

"And when the dance was over he kept hold of her hand and led her over to where her cousin was standin', and says he, 'Madam, the minister is in the next room, and with your leave there'll be a wedding here to-night.' And Miss Amaryllis tried to pull her hand out of his, and she was laughin' and blushin', and everybody come crowdin' around to see what was the matter, and she says, 'Let go my hand, Hamilton. Wait till I go home, and I'll marry you.' And he laughed and says he, 'You haven't any home to go to. The Cedars belongs to me, and we might as well be married here.' And she says, 'Well, let me go up-stairs and put on a white dress.'

"They said she had on a yeller silk, jest the color of her hair, with white lace on the waist and sleeves and a string o' pearls around her neck. And Hamilton jest held on to her hand still tighter. And she says, 'Hamilton, you hurt my hand; please let go.' And he says, 'I wouldn't hurt you for worlds, but I'm going to hold your hand till the minister pronounces us man and wife.' And he put his thumb and finger together,

COURTSHIP OF MISS AMARYLLIS

jest so, around her wrist like a bracelet, and says he, 'That can't hurt you. Now choose your bridesmaids, and we'll call the minister in and be married at once.' Says he, 'I always intended that my bride should wear yellow silk.' And one o' the gyirls says, 'But she must take off the pearl necklace; pearls at a wedding mean tears.' And Hamilton says, 'Let it alone; every pearl stands for a tear of joy.' And then he looked around and says he, 'I want four groomsmen.' And the young man that Miss Amaryllis was about to dance with when Hamilton come in, he spoke up and says he, 'I'd rather be the bridegroom, but if I can't be that, I'll be first groomsman.' And three other young men, they said they'd be groomsmen, too. And they all stood up, and the preacher come in, and he married 'em jest as solemn as if they'd been in church.

"They said it was right curious, how they'd been fiddlin' and dancin' and carryin' on, but the minute the preacher stepped into the room everybody was as still as death. I've heard folks say that they always felt like laughin' when they oughtn't to laugh, at a funeral or a communion service or a babtizin', but, child, when a man and a woman stands up side by side and the preacher begins to say the words that binds 'em together

THE LAND OF LONG AGO

for life, nobody ever feels like laughin' then. A weddin', honey, is the solemnest thing in the world, and they said before the preacher got through sayin' the ceremony over Hamilton and Miss Amaryllis, there was tears in nearly everybody's eyes, and when he stooped down to kiss the bride, it was so still you could hear the little screech-owls in the woods at the side o' the house. And Hamilton turned around and bowed to the first groomsman and says he, ' Sir, I robbed you of your partner a while ago, now I give her back to you for the next dance'; and he took hold o' the first bridesmaid's hand and motioned to the fiddlers to begin playin', and they struck up a tune and everybody went to dancin' as if life wasn't made for anything but pleasure. And the next mornin', Hamilton and his bride started for home, ridin' horseback and stoppin' along the way as they come to taverns or their friends' houses, and folks said they looked like they'd found the pot of gold at the foot o' the rainbow."

Aunt Jane began rolling up her knitting, a sure sign that the story was ended. But even the tales of childhood went farther than this. It was not enough to know " and so they were married "; I must hear also how they " lived happily ever afterward."

COURTSHIP OF MISS AMARYLLIS

"Oh! go on," I cried; "this can't be the end of the story."

"Sometimes it's best not to know the end of a story," said Aunt Jane gravely.

But I heeded not the warning. I must know more of this girl who drew to herself the love of men as the ocean draws the rivers. "Tell me a little more about Miss Amaryllis," I pleaded.

But Aunt Jane was silent, and her eyes were sad. "There's mighty little more to tell," she said at last, her words coming slowly and reluctantly. "Miss Amaryllis died when her baby was born. The baby died, too, and they buried both of 'em in the same grave. It was the dead o' winter, and one o' the coldest winters we'd had for years. The ground was froze solid as a rock, and the snow was nearly a foot deep. It's hard enough, child, to lay the dead in the ground when the sun's shinin' and the earth's warm and there's plenty of sweet flowers and green sod to cover the grave with. But when it comes to cuttin' a grave in the snow and the ice and layin' away the body of a child that's bone of your bone and flesh of your flesh, or maybe a husband or a wife that's nearer and dearer yet, why, there's no words, I reckon, that can tell what a trial that is.

THE LAND OF LONG AGO

I always used to pray that my funerals might come in the spring or summer when everything was warm and pretty, and, child, my prayer was answered. I never had a winter funeral. I ricollect my baby brother dyin' when I was jest a little child. It was towards the end o' winter, and the first night after the funeral it rained, a hard, cold, beatin' rain, and mother walked the floor all night and wrung her hands and cried at the thought of her child's body lyin' in the grave and the cold rain fallin' on it; and she never got riconciled to the child's death and able to sleep right, till spring come and the grass got green, and she could carry flowers and put 'em on its little grave.

"And that's the way Hamilton Schuyler was, only worse. He had the body dressed in the dress she was wearin' at the dance the night he married her, and when they put the corpse in the coffin in the big parlor, he stayed by it for three days and nights, leanin' over and whisperin' and smilin' and smoothin' her hair and pattin' the little dead baby on its hands and face. Every time they'd say anything about buryin' the body, he'd throw his arms around the coffin and carry on so terrible that there was nothin' to do but let him have his way. He kept sayin', 'Maybe she's not dead. She may be sleepin' like the baby, and to-morrow they'll both wake up.' And then he'd say, 'If it was only summer-time! Can't you find some roses? She ought to have her hands full of roses.'

"And as soon as dark come, he'd have all the wax candles lighted in the parlor, and they said it made your flesh creep to hear him talkin' and laughin' with the dead all night long, and the whole room blazin' with light jest like there was a weddin' goin' on.

"Well, when the third day come, they said the funeral had to be, and they dug the grave in the family buryin'-ground and cut branches of cedar and pine and lined it so you couldn't see the frozen earth anywhere, and they covered the coffin with ivy off the walls o' the old house. It was one o' these clear, sunshiny winter days, when the sky's soft and blue jest like it is in May or June, but the air was bitter cold, and there was a crust of ice on top o' the snow and the frozen ground under it. Hamilton had got kind o' quiet by this time, and he was so weak from loss o' sleep and not eatin' anything that they thought they wouldn't have any more trouble, but when they let the coffin down into the ground and the first clod fell on it, it took the

THE LAND OF LONG AGO

strength of three men to keep Hamilton from throwin' himself into the grave."

Alas, the sad, sad story, beginning with love and spring and youth, and ending beside an open grave under wintry skies! Aunt Jane was wiping her glasses, and my tears were flowing fast.

"Death has mighty few terrors when it comes at the right time, honey," said Aunt Jane tremulously. "You know the Bible says 'We all do fade as a leaf'; and when a person's lived out his app'inted time, three score years and ten, or maybe four score, why, his death is jest like the fallin' of a leaf. It's had its spring and its summer, and it's nothin' to cry about when the frost comes and touches it, and it falls to the ground to make room for the new leaves that'll come next spring. But jest suppose that the leaves fell as soon as the trees got green and pretty in the springtime, and suppose all the roses died in the bud. Wouldn't this be a sorrowful world, if things was that way? There ain't any bitterness in the tears that's shed over old folks' coffins, but when I think o' Miss Amaryllis dyin' the way she did, before she'd lived her life and had the happiness she ought to 'a' had, I feel like questionin' the ways o' Providence. And then, again, I think maybe she had as

COURTSHIP OF MISS AMARYLLIS

much happiness in that one year as most folks has in a lifetime. It ain't often a man loves a woman so much that he can't live without her, but that's the way Hamilton Schuyler loved Miss Amaryllis, and that's the main reason why I ricollect her so well after all these years. Her hair and her eyes would keep me from forgittin' her outright, and when I think of how she looked and how Hamilton Schuyler loved her, it seems like she was different from all the other women that ever I've known."

"Dust and ashes! Dust and ashes!" sings the poet; but "Love and beauty! Love and beauty!" answers the soul. And thus, doubly immortalized, and radiant as when she played with the hearts of men in her golden youth, this maiden more beautiful than her name shall live in the tale I tell as it was told to me.

"You ricollect the Bible says 'Love is strong as death,'" said Aunt Jane, "but that ain't always so. You'll see a husband or a wife die, and you'll think the one that's left never will git over grievin' for the one that's gone, and the first thing you know there's a second marriage, and that shows that death is stronger than love, and I reckon it's well that it's so. If one's taken and the other's left, it's because the livin' has got a

THE LAND OF LONG AGO

work to do in this world. They can't spend their lives grievin' after the dead, and they oughtn't to try to foller the dead. But once in a while, honey, it's a good thing to find a love that's stronger than death. 'Many waters cannot quench love, neither can the floods drown it.'"

The tremulous old voice ceased again and there was a long silence. At last, "What became of Hamilton Schuyler?" I asked softly.

Aunt Jane roused herself with a start. She also had known a love that was stronger than death, and her thoughts were not with Hamilton and Miss Amaryllis.

"Hamilton?" she said dreamily. "Oh, yes! Poor man! Poor man! It was all they could do to make him come away from the grave, and when they got him home and tried to persuade him to go to bed and take some rest, he'd throw out his arms and push 'em away and say, 'There's no more rest for me on this earth. How can a man get into his bed and sleep, when his wife and child are lyin' out in the frozen ground?' And for weeks he'd go out to the graveyard in the dead o' the night and wander up and down the house like a ghost. He stayed around the place till spring come, and when the flowers begun to bloom he got worse instead o' better. It looked like every flower and tree reminded him of Miss Amaryllis. And he'd walk down the gyarden lookin' at her rose-bushes and talkin' to himself, and every time a rose bloomed, he'd gether it and put it on her grave. And one mornin', about the last o' May, he told one o' the slaves to saddle his horse, and when they asked him where he was goin', he said: 'I'm going to find her. I found her once, and I can find her again.'

"They tried to reason with him, but they might as well 'a' talked to the air. He rode off like mad, and the next folks heard of him, he was 'way off yonder in some foreign country; and after a while the news come that he'd been found dead in his bed. Whether he grieved himself to death or whether he took his own life nobody ever knew. I ricollect how glad I was when I heard about it, for I knew he'd found Miss Amaryllis.

"But there's one thing, child, that troubles me and always has troubled me, especially since Abram died. You know that text that says there's neither marryin' nor givin' in marriage in heaven, but we'll all be like the angels? I've thought and thought about that text, but I can't see how a man and a woman that's loved each other and lived together as husband and wife for a lifetime in this world can ever be anything but husband and wife, no matter what other world they go to nor how long death's kept 'em parted from each other; and when death comes between 'em at the very beginnin', it looks like they ought to have their happiness in heaven. I know it's wrong to go against the words o' the Bible, and yet I can't help hopin' and trustin' that somehow or other Hamilton Schuyler found his wife and the little child that never drew a breath in this world; for that was all the heaven he wanted, and it looks like he had a right to it."

Does it call for laughter or for tears, this splendid audacity of the soul that gives us strength to stand among the wrecks of human life and in the face of inexorable law plead our right to love and happiness? And yet, is not inexorable law, but another name for the eternal justice that measures out to every man his just deserts? And who but the fool dare say that eternal justice is but a dream?

For "now abideth faith, hope, love, these three;

but the greatest of these is love." And if faith and hope fail not, surely the love that is stronger than death shall one day find its own, and hold its own through all eternity.

IV
AUNT JANE GOES A-VISITING

IV

AUNT JANE GOES A-VISITING

"YES," said Aunt Jane, "I've been up to Lexin'ton to see Henrietta, and I jest got home day before yesterday. Set down, child, and I'll tell you all about it."

The old lady's eyes were sparkling with happiness, a faint flush was in her cheeks, and she looked as if

THE LAND OF LONG AGO

she had drunk from that fount that all are seeking and that none has ever found.

"Henrietta's been wantin' me to visit her for many a year back," she went on; "but I've been puttin' it off, one way or another, like old folks always do when young folks wants 'em to do anything that's for their good. But you see I've lived right here in this old house pretty near all my life, and takin' me up and carryin' me to off to Lexin'ton was jest about like takin' up that old ellum-tree out yonder and carryin' it over and settin' it out in another county. You've got to be mighty keerful how you move old folks around. However, I've been and come back again, and I ain't any the worse for it, and Henrietta's satisfied because she's had her way. Henrietta used to live in Danville, you know, but Archibald — that's her husband — sold out and moved to Lexin'ton about a year ago, and he's built her a house the like o' which never was seen in the bluegrass region, so they say. And as soon as they moved into it, Henrietta wrote to me and says, 'Grandma, I'm not goin' to ask you to come to see me. But next week Archibald and I will be down, and we're goin' to take you home with us whether you want to go or not.'"

AUNT JANE GOES A-VISITING

Aunt Jane's laugh had a ring of pride, for the love of this favorite grandchild was very dear to her.

"And, honey," she said confidentially, "that was the only thing that made me go. If Henrietta had kept on jest askin' me to come to see her, I'd 'a' kept on holdin' back. I know Henrietta loves me, but whenever she'd say anything about me goin' to see her, I'd think to myself, ' Now, Henrietta's jest askin' me because she thinks I'll feel bad if she don't; and, like as not, if I was to go up there amongst all her fine friends, she'd be ashamed of me.' But when she said she was comin' to take me back with her, I says to myself, ' I'll go, for I know Henrietta wants me.'

"Henrietta was mightily afraid the ride on the cyars would tire me out; but I don't reckon goin' to heaven'll be any easier and pleasanter to me than goin' to Lexin'ton that June day. It looked like everything was fixed to suit me. The weather was jest the kind I like, and the seats in the cyar was as comfortable as any chair I ever set in, and I jest leaned back and looked out o' the winder and thought about the times when I'd ride to town with father, when I was a little child, and father'd take care of me and p'int out the sights to me like Henrietta and Archibald did that day.

THE LAND OF LONG AGO

"I reckon Kentuckians are the biggest fools in the world over their own State. Sam Amos used to say if you'd set a born-and-bred Kentuckian down in the Gyarden of Eden he'd begin to brag about his farm over in the blue-grass; and you jest ride from here to Lexin'ton about the first o' June, what Abram used to call 'clover and blue-grass time,' and if you are a Kentuckian, you'll thank God, and if you ain't a Kentuckian, you'll wish you was.

"There's a heap of good to be got out of travelin', honey. One thing is, I won't have to go back thirty or forty years to find somethin' to talk about when you come to see me. Even if I hadn't seen Henriétta or Henrietta's home, the things I saw on the way from here to Lexin'ton will keep me talkin' the rest o' my days and make me happier jest to think of 'em. Such farms and hills and trees and orchards, and such level corn-fields, oat-fields and pretty rollin' land in between 'em I know can't be seen anywhere but in Kentucky.

"I couldn't help thinkin' of old man Mose Elrod. His farm j'ined the Amos farm, and a better piece o' land you couldn't 'a' found; but he had a cousin down in Texas, and the cousin kept writin' to him

AUNT JANE GOES A-VISITING

about the soil o' Texas and the climate o' Texas and the money there was to be made there, till finally old man Mose got the Texas fever and sold out and moved down in the neighborhood o' San Antonio. Every now and then he'd write home, and from what he said we judged he was prosperin' and feelin' contented in his new home; but in about a year and a half here he come, walkin' in and takin' the neighbors by surprise. He went all over the neighborhood shakin' hands and tellin' folks how glad he was to be back again. Says he, 'I've been homesick night and day for eighteen months, and all the money in Texas couldn't keep me away from Kentucky any longer.'

"He said he set up all night on the cyars so's the conductor would tell him when he got on Kentucky soil, and the nearer he got home the happier he got, and when the brakeman hollered, 'Muldraughs Hill!' he jumped up, threw up his hat, and hollered, 'Glory! Hallelujah!' Of course the passengers was skeered, and one man says, 'Search him and see if he's got any weapons on him,' and the conductor come runnin' up, and old man Mose says, 'I haven't got any weapons, conductor, and I'm not drunk nor crazy, but I've been down in Texas for a year and a half, and I'm jest happy

THE LAND OF LONG AGO

over gittin' back home.' And the conductor says: 'Well, that's excuse enough for anything. Holler as loud as you please; you sha'n't be put off the train.'

"The old man said he could 'a' stood it if there'd been any knobs or hills or big trees. But he said that prairie land nearly run him crazy, especially in the evenin'. He said he'd watch the sun goin' down like a ball o' fire away off across that level prairie, and he'd think about how the sunset looked in Kentucky, with old Pilot Knob and Prewitt's Knob loomin' up on the horizon, and he'd drop his head in his hands and cry like a baby.

"And talkin' about sunsets, child, reminds me of a picture in Henrietta's parlor. There never was anything like the inside o' Henrietta's home. Her and Archibald went all over Europe when they was first married, and everywhere they went they gethered up pictures and marble images and such things, and whichever way you'd turn there was somethin' to look at that you never'd seen before. And when you've been livin' all your life in a house like this old farmhouse o' mine, it gives you a curious sort o' feelin' to be set down all at once in a place like Henrietta's. Why, for two or three days I hardly knew the name of

AUNT JANE GOES A-VISITING

anything I was eatin' or drinkin' or lookin' at or walkin' on or settin' on, and when I try to ricollect the different rooms, I git 'em all mixed up. But there's one thing that's jest as clear as day in my mind, and that is the picture I'm tellin' you about. The name of it was ' The Angelus.' Now ain't that a pretty name? — ' The Angelus.' Why, it sounds jest like music. The minute I come across it, I stopped still in front of it and looked and looked and looked. And says I, ' Child, this picture makes me feel like sayin' my prayers.' And Henrietta laughed, and says she, ' Grandma, that's jest what the people in the picture are doin'.' And she said that over yonder in France, in some o' the places out in the country, places pretty much like our Goshen neighborhood, I reckon, they was in the habit o' ringin' the church bells at sundown, and when people heard the bells, they'd stop whatever they was doin' and say their prayers. And she told me all about the man that painted ' The Angelus,' how poor he was, and how folks laughed at his pictures, and wouldn't buy 'em because he painted things jest as they was, plain and natural. She said her picture was a copy of the one he painted, and when she saw how much I liked it, she says, ' Grandma, I'm goin' to get you a copy of " The

THE LAND OF LONG AGO

Angelus,"' and I says, 'No, child, I ain't one o' the kind that has to have a picture o' the folks and the things they love. I've got that picture right in my old brain, and all I have to do to see it is jest to shut my eyes and it'll come — the sunset and the field and the two people prayin' and the bell, — I'll hear that, too, ringin' jest like the old bell that used to ring in Goshen church.' Every day I'd go into the parlor at Henrietta's about the time the sun'd be goin' down, and I'd look first at the sunset in the sky and then at the sunset in the picture, and I couldn't tell which was the prettiest.

"Uncle Jim Matthews used to say that every church bell said, 'Get up, get up, and go to church!' And in them days people minded the church bell. But nowadays it looks like the only bells folks pays any attention to is the breakfast-bell and the dinner-bell and the supper-bell. And I've been thinkin', honey, what a blessed thing it would be, if, all over the world, folks could hear a bell ringin' at sundown and callin' on everybody to stop their work or their pleasure and fold their hands for a minute and pray. Why, the prayers would go up to heaven like the birds flyin' home to their nests, and jest think how many wrong things would

AUNT JANE GOES A-VISITING

be stopped. If a murderer was liftin' his hand, that bell would be like a voice from the sky, sayin', 'Thou shalt not kill.' If a husband and wife was quarrelin', and they heard the Angelus, and stopped to pray, why, maybe, after they'd prayed they'd kiss and make up. Yes, child, the Angelus would do a heap o' good. But if anybody's once looked at the picture, they won't need the bell. I know I'll never see the sun settin' behind them knobs over yonder that I won't think o' that picture, and whatever I'm doin' I'll have to stop and fold my hands and bow my head, the same as I used to do when Parson Page'd stand up in the old Goshen church and say, 'Let us pray.'

"Here's a picture o' Henrietta's house, child. I knew I couldn't tell folks about it so's they'd have any idea o' what it was, so I brought this picture." And she handed me a photograph of one of those modern palaces which, under the spells of the two master magicians, Art and Wealth, are springing up on the soil of the New South to replace the worn-out mansions of ante-bellum days.

"When I looked at Henrietta's house," continued Aunt Jane, "I thought o' what Uncle Billy Bascom used to say. Uncle Billy's the kind that can't enjoy this world for thinkin' about the next one. He's spent his life preparin' for death, and it looks like it hurts him to see anybody gittin' any pleasure out o' the things o' this world. Every time any o' the Goshen folks'd put up a house that was a little bit better than what Uncle Billy'd been used to, he'd shake his head and say, 'Yes, Lord; folks can make theirselves so comfortable here on this earth that they won't have a thought about gittin' a clear title to a mansion in the skies.'

"And that house o' Henrietta's was enough to make anybody forget about their mansion in the skies. Henrietta's havin' her heaven now, and she'll have it hereafter, and Archibald, too. For the 'cares o' the world and the deceitfulness o' riches' hasn't choked any o' the good seed that's been sown in their hearts. How many young folks do you reckon would think o' comin' down here and takin' a old woman like me home with 'em, and treatin' her like a queen, and showin' her all the sights in a place like Lexin'ton?

"Archibald named 'em all over to me, and Henrietta says, 'Now where do you want to go first, grandma?' And I says: 'I want to see Henry Clay's house. Take me there first, and I don't care whether I see any o' the rest o' the sights or not.' So the next day Henrietta

AUNT JANE GOES A-VISITING

took me to Ashland, the place where Henry Clay had lived, and I saw the bed he slept in and the table he wrote on and the inkstand and the pen he used. And I says to myself, 'I'm in Henry Clay's home. Henry Clay! — the man I used to hear my father talk about when I was a young gyirl — the man that'd rather be in the right than to be President.' And I ricollected the time Henry Clay spoke in town and father went to hear him, and when he got back home, mother asked him what kind of a man Henry Clay was. And father says, says he, 'Henry Clay ain't a man'; and mother laughed (she was used to father's way o' talkin'), and says she, 'Well, if he ain't a man, what is he?' And father studied a minute, and then he says, 'Do you ricollect the tongues o' fire that descended on the apostles on the day of Pentecost?' Says he, 'If one o' them tongues o' fire was put in the body of a man, that'd be Henry Clay.' Says he, 'He stands up and runs his eye over the crowd, and from that minute he's got every man there right in the holler of his hand, and he does jest what he pleases with 'em; and if he looks any particular man in the face, that man'll feel like he's in the presence of his Maker.'

"Father never got over Clay not bein' President;

and whenever anybody'd talk about it, he'd shake his head and say, 'There's somethin' wrong with the times when a man like Henry Clay can't git the Presidency.'

"Now, here I am, child, 'way back in Henry Clay's time, when I set out to tell you about my visit to Henrietta's. That wanderin' o' the mind is a pretty good sign of old age, I reckon, but I 'most always manage to ricollect where I started from and where I'm goin' to.

"Well, as soon as I got to feelin' at home Henrietta says, 'Now, grandma, I'm goin' to give you a reception and introduce you to my friends.' And I says: 'Honey, you'd better not do that. You know I'm jest a old-fashioned woman, and maybe I wouldn't know how to behave at a reception.' And Henrietta laughed, and says she, 'All in the world you have to do, grandma, is to shake hands with the people and be glad to see 'em.'

"And, sure enough, it was jest that way. Everybody was smilin' and sayin' they was glad to see me, and that reception was pretty much like shakin' hands with your neighbors after prayer-meetin' and church, only there was more of 'em.

AUNT JANE GOES A-VISITING

"I started to wear my black alpaca to the reception, but Henrietta says, 'No, grandma, I've had a dress made especially for you.' Jest wait a minute, honey, and I'll get that dress."

And when she appeared a moment later her face wore the radiant look of a girl who displays her first party costume, or a bride her wedding-gown. Over her arm hung the reception gown of soft, black China silk, with plain full skirt and shirred waist. There were ruffles of point lace in the full sleeves, and she held up the point-lace cap and fichu that completed the costume.

"To think o' me wearin' such clothes," said Aunt Jane exultingly. "And the curious part of it was, child, that I hadn't had these things on five minutes, till I felt like they belonged to me, and it seemed as if I'd been wearin' lace and silk all my life. And Henrietta stood off and looked at me, and says she, 'Grandma, you look exactly like a family portrait.' And when Archibald come home after the reception, he says, says he, 'We ought to have grandma's picture painted in that dress.' And Henrietta says, 'Yes; and I want another picture of grandma in her old purple calico dress and gingham apron, settin' in that old high-back rockin'-chair with one of her patchwork quilts over her lap.' Says she, 'That's the way I remember seein' grandma when I was a little gyirl, and that's the way *I* want her picture taken.'"

She paused to shake out the lustrous silk and spread the fichu over it that I might see the delicate pattern of the lace.

"I started to leave this dress at Henrietta's," she observed, "for I knew I wouldn't have use for such clothes as these down here on the farm, but Henrietta folded 'em up and put 'em in my trunk, and she said I had to wear 'em every Sunday evenin' and sit out on the porch and think about her and Archibald. And then, child, when I die they can bury me in this dress." And her cheerful smile told me that if death had held any terrors for Aunt Jane, those terrors would be largely assuaged by the thought of going to her long rest in point lace and silk. Nigh on to eighty years, "but yet a woman!"

"Now what was the next thing I went to? Oh, yes! the Brownin' Club. Two or three days after the reception, Henrietta says to me, 'Grandma, the Brownin' Club meets with me this evenin', and I want you to put on your silk dress and come down to the parlor and listen to our papers.' And she told me who

AUNT JANE GOES A-VISITING

Brownin' was, and said she was goin' to read a paper on his home life.

"Well, I thought to myself that there wasn't much hope o' me understandin' anything I'd hear at that Brownin' Club, but of course I was glad to dress up again in my silk dress and my lace, and to please Henrietta I went down into the parlor and listened to the readin'. First, a young lady read a paper about the 'Message of Brownin'.' She said every poet had a message to give to the world jest like the prophets in Old-Testament times, and I gethered from her paper that Brownin' was a man that always looked on the bright side and believed that things was goin' to come right in the end; and towards the last she read some mighty pretty verses. I wish I could ricollect 'em all. It was somethin' about the spring o' the year and the mornin' and the dew like pearls and the birds flyin'. The words was jest like a picture of a spring mornin', and the last of it was, ' God's in his heaven — all's right with the world!' That's jest as true as anything in the Bible, and it sounds like it might 'a' come out o' the Bible, don't it, child?

"Then another lady read some o' Brownin's poetry, 'Pary—' somethin' or other."

125

THE LAND OF LONG AGO

"Paracelsus," I suggested.

"That's it," said Aunt Jane, "but I ain't a bit wiser than I was before, for I never did find out whether that was the name of a man or a woman or a town or a river or what. I set and listened, and every now and then it'd seem like there was somethin' that I could understand, but before I could lay hold of it here'd come a lot o' big words that I never heard tell of before, and, I declare to goodness, my old brains got tired tryin' to git some sense out o' that poetry. Why, it was jest like tryin' to read at night by the light o' the fire. The fire'll blaze up, and you'll see everything plain for a minute, and then it'll die down, and there you are in the dark again.

"Well, when the lady got through readin' the poetry, she said she was goin' to read her interpretation of it. I ricollected how Joseph interpreted Pharaoh's dream and Daniel interpreted Nebuchadnezzar's dream, and I says to myself, 'Now, I'll find out all about it.' But bless your life, child, the poetry was hard enough to understand, but the interpretation was a heap harder; and I says to myself, 'Brownin's poetry never was intended for a old woman like me.' And I jest leaned back in my chair and looked at the

AUNT JANE GOES A-VISITING

hats and the bonnets the ladies had on. Pretty clothes always was one o' my weak points, and will be till I die, I reckon. When I was a child father used to question us children about the sermon when we got home from church. I never could tell much about it, except the text, and I ricollect hearin' mother say to him one Sunday, ' If Jane could jest remember as much about the sermon as she remembers about the hats and bonnets, we could have her ordained to preach.'

"There was one hat I saw at the Brownin' Club that I'll ricollect as long as I ricollect ' The Angelus.' It was made out o' white lace and trimmed with pink roses that made me think o' the roses in my weddin'-bonnet, only they was buds and these was full-blown ones, so full-blown that it looked like they was ready to shatter and fall if the wind blew on 'em, and so natural you could almost smell 'em. I declare, that hat made me wish I was a young gyirl again.

"Then Henrietta read her paper, and it was jest as pretty a story as ever I listened to; about him fallin' in love with that sick woman that hadn't walked a step for years, and how he married her against her father's will, and took her 'way off to Florence, the same place where Henrietta and Archibald went when they was in Europe, and where Henrietta got that quilt pattern for me. And she told how kind he was to her, and how he'd git up in the mornin' and gether roses and put 'em by her bed so they'd be the first things she'd look at when she opened her eyes. And thinks I to myself, 'Most men wants a woman that can cook for 'em and sew for 'em and clean up after 'em, and Brownin' must 'a' been a mighty good man to marry a woman that couldn't do anything for him but jest love him.' Somehow I can't git the thought o' Brownin' out o' my head. He must 'a' been mighty different from the common run o' men, and his life don't need interpretin' like his poetry does.

"Maybe you wonder, honey, how a old woman like me could enjoy bein' at a Brownin' Club, and I reckon I was as much out o' place as mother's old spinnin'-wheel that Henrietta had in one corner of her parlor along with all that fine furniture and the fine things she'd brought from Europe. But, then, I couldn't feel a bit bad, for there set Henrietta, my child's child; she had everything I hadn't had, and I jest laughed to myself, and thinks I, 'I'm livin' again in my children and my grandchildren, and I ain't missed a thing.'"

Aunt Jane paused for breath and leaned back in her

AUNT JANE GOES A-VISITING

chair, smiling and smoothing down her gingham apron. I waited in silence, for I knew that the near memories of her visit to her beloved grandchild were as vivid and interesting to her as the far memories of girlhood and young womanhood, and the tide of recollections would soon flow again.

"Well, the next thing we went to was a big meetin' of women from all sorts o' clubs. When Henrietta told me what it was, I says to myself, 'Now, I'll see if what Uncle Billy Bascom told me is the truth or not.' Uncle Billy'd been sent up to the legislature twice from our district, and when I heard he'd been elected the second time, I couldn't help thinkin' about what Sam Amos used to say, that when folks got tired seein' a man around and wanted to git shed of him a while, they always sent him to the legislature. That's about the way it was with Uncle Billy.

"Me and Uncle Billy has always been good friends, and after he got back home he come around to see me, and when we'd shook hands and inquired about each other's health, he looked me right in the face and says he, 'Jane, I've been to Sodom and Gomorrah.' And says I, 'Uncle Billy, that's about the hardest thing ever I heard said about a Kentucky legislature, and I've heard some pretty hard things in my day and time.' And says he: 'No, Jane; you misunderstand me. I ain't referrin' to the legislature; the legislature's all right.' Says he: 'We set sixty days and drawed our pay regular, and we passed pretty nigh a hundred bills, and might 'a' passed that many more if we'd kept on settin'; but as the constitution don't permit us to set longer, why, of course, we had to adjourn and come on home, leavin' a good deal o' business unfinished. No,' says he, ' it ain't the legislature I'm talkin' about, it's the women, the women.' Says he: 'There was a time when it was some pleasure for a man to go up to the legislature. Us men, we'd git together and resolute, and debate, and pass our bills, and everything'd go off as smooth as satin. Now and then we might git a disturbin' sort of a letter from some o' the home folks about somethin' we'd been doin' that didn't suit 'em, a dog-tax or somethin' o' that sort, but they'd be too fur to worry us much. But,' says he, 'the way the women has got to carryin' on, if it wasn't for the pay and the honor o' the thing, I'd ruther stay right here on my farm than to go up yonder to Frankfort and rastle with a lot o' women that's strayed so far from the footsteps o' their mothers and grandmothers that nothin'

AUNT JANE GOES A-VISITING

but a miracle could bring 'em back.' Says he: 'We could hardly pass a bill in any peace whatsoever, for them women. If we set out to give a little money to the State College, why, here'd come a delegation o' women from Lexin'ton wantin' to know whether the gyirls would git their share of it.' Says he: 'There ain't a right or a privilege goin' that they don't want to cut it half in two, and give the littlest half to us men and keep the biggest half for the women; some of 'em even goes so far as to say that women ought to vote. And,' says he, 'they've got to clubbin' together, and what one woman can't think of, the others can; and there was hardly a man in the legislature that wasn't pestered with havin' to look after some sort o' bill that'd been hatched up in one o' these here clubs. I got so outdone with 'em,' says he, 'that whenever a bill'd come up, I'd say to whoever was settin' by me, "Has the women got anything to do with it?" And if they had, I'd vote against it, and if they hadn't, I'd vote for it. One o' their bills,' says he, 'sounded mighty reasonable, the "forestry bill," they called it, but it never come up.' Says he, 'We had a little redistricting to do for the benefit o' the party, and made a few new offices jest to please the people, and betwixt this and that,' says he, 'we didn't git round to the forestry bill.' Says he, 'I might 'a' supported that, if it had come up, but then I don't know but what after all it'd 'a' been a dangerous sort o' thing.' Says he: 'The more you give a woman the more she wants. We give women their property rights, and now they're wantin' to vote and to manage the schools and the 'sylums and pretty near everything else. And,' says he, 'if we was to pass that there forestry bill, like as not the first thing you know, a man'd have to git a permit from some o' these women's clubs before he could chop a piece o' kindlin'-wood in his own back yard.'

"And then the old man went on to tell how he went up to Lexin'ton after the legislature was over, and that was what he meant by goin' to Sodom and Gomorrah. Says he, 'There's women up there, Jane, that don't know a water-bucket from a churn, and if you was to show 'em a potater-patch in full bloom, they'd think it was some sort of a flower-gyarden.' Says he, 'The clubs was more numerous than the children, and it looks to me like the race is dyin' out, dyin' out, Jane; and maybe it's jest as well,' says he, 'for there ain't any women nowadays like the old-time ones, for instance, my mother and grandmother,' says he."

AUNT JANE GOES A-VISITING

Aunt Jane broke off with a laugh. "I knew as soon as he started out that he was comin' to his mother and grandmother. Uncle Billy couldn't talk twenty minutes with anybody without tellin' 'em how his mother had fifteen children, and cooked and sewed and washed and ironed for 'em all, and how his grandmother was one o' the women that carried water at Bryan's Station, and how she fought a wildcat one night on the Wilderness Road when her husband was away killin' some game for their supper.

"Well, I went to this club meetin', I can't ricollect jest what Henrietta called it, but it seems they had got together to tell about all the work they'd done in the past year, and plan out their next year's work.

"There was one lady I took particular notice of. I thought she was a married woman, but I heard 'em callin' her 'Miss Laura,' and I found out afterwards that she was an old maid. In my day, child, you could tell an old maid the minute you set eyes on her. But nowadays the old maids and the married women looks about alike, and one's jest as happy and good lookin' and busy and well contented as the other, and folks seem to think jest as much of the old maids as they do of the married women. I said somethin' o' this sort to Henrietta, and she laughed and says, 'Yes, grandma; the old maids nowadays have their hands so full lookin' after the rights o' the married women and the little children that they don't have time to grow old or worry about not bein' married, and of course,' says she, 'we can't help lovin' 'em and lookin' up to 'em when they're so good and so useful.'

"But, as I was sayin', this Miss Laura told how her club had worked for ten years to git married women their rights, so's a married woman could own her own property and manage it to suit herself and have the spendin' of her own wages while she lived and make a will when she come to die. And that made me think o' Sally Ann's experience and pore 'Lizabeth. And Miss Laura says, 'But there's one right still that a married woman hasn't got, and that is the right to her own children.' And she told how the law give the father a right to take a child away from its mother and carry it off whenever he pleased, and bring it up as he pleased and app'int its guardians. And she told how many times they'd been to the legislature to git the law changed, and said they'd have to keep on goin' till they got this right for mothers, jest like they'd got property rights for wives. And I thought of Uncle

AUNT JANE GOES A-VISITING

Billy's grandmother, and says I to myself: 'Don't you reckon a legislature's jest as terrifyin' to a woman as wildcats and Indians? Ain't these women got jest as much courage as their grandmothers?'

"One lady got up and told what they was doin' to keep the fine trees from bein' all cut down, jest like Uncle Billy said, and that reminded me of Abram. A tree was like a brother to Abram. He was always plantin' trees, but I never knew him to cut one down unless it was dyin' or dead. You see that big sugar-maple out yonder by the fence, child? Well, right beside it there used to be a big silver poplar. There ain't a prettier tree in the world than the silver poplar. It's pretty in the sunshine and it's still prettier by night, if the moon's shinin'; and when the wind's blowin', why, I can sit and look at that tree by the hour. But it's got a bad way o' sproutin' from the root, and the young trees come up everywhere and crowd out everything else, jest like people that ain't content with their own land and always covetin' other folks' farms. Well, I got so tired o' choppin' down the young sprouts every spring and summer that I told Abram that tree had to go, and, besides, it was sp'ilin' the shape o' the young sugar-maple right by it. I reckon Abram

THE LAND OF LONG AGO

had got tired, too, hearin' me quarrel about the sprouts comin' up in my flower-beds, so he went out to the wood-shed and got his ax. He stopped a minute on the front porch and looked up at the tree, and jest then a little breeze sprung up and every leaf blew wrong side out. And Abram laid down his ax and says he: 'Jane, I can't do it. I'll cut the sprouts down, but don't ask me to cut down a tree that looks that way when the wind blows.' And the old poplar stood, honey, till it was struck by lightnin' one summer, and died at the top. Then Abram was willin' to have it cut down.

"What was I talkin' about, honey? Oh, yes; them women's clubs. Well, I set there listenin' to 'em tellin' how their clubs had worked for this thing and that, and how hard it was to git men to see things the way they saw 'em, and it come over me all at once that they was contendin' with the same sort o' troubles us women down in Goshen had when we got our organ and our cyarpet for the church. I ricollect when we was talkin' about the cyarpet Silas Petty says: 'What's the use o' havin' that cyarpet? Hasn't this church got along fifteen years with jest these good pine boards underfoot?' And Sally Ann says: 'Yes; you men folks

AUNT JANE GOES A-VISITING

think that because things has always been thus and so, they've always got to be. But,' says she, ' I've noticed that when a thing always has been, most likely it's a thing that ought never to 'a' been.' And from what I could gether, listenin' to the ladies read their papers, there was the same old trouble betwixt the clubs and the legislatures that there used to be down in Goshen church, the women wantin' to go on, and the men pullin' back and standin' still.

"And one lady told about Emperor William over yonder in Germany sayin' that women oughtn't to do anything but cook and go to church and nurse the children, and says I, 'That's Silas Petty over again.' And then she went on to tell how some o' the men was findin' fault with women because families wasn't as large as they was in their great-grandmothers' day. And thinks I to myself, 'That's jest like old man Bob Crawford.'

"Well, one after another they'd stand up and tell about all the good works their clubs had done, sendin' books to the mountain people, tryin' to make better schools for the children, and havin' laws made to keep women and little children from bein' worked to death in factories and mills, and I declare, child, it reminded me more of an old-fashioned experience meetin' than anything I could think of, and says I to myself: 'Why, Uncle Billy's all wrong. This ain't Sodom and Gomorrah; it's the comin' of the kingdom of God on earth.' And when the meetin' was about to break, Henrietta got up and says, 'Grandma, the ladies want you to make them a speech'; and I jest laughed right out and says I: 'Why, honey, I can't make a speech. Who ever heard of a old woman like me makin' a speech?'

"And Henrietta says, 'Well, tell us, grandma, what you've been thinkin' about us and about our work while you've been sittin' here listenin' to us talk.' And I says, 'Well, if that's makin' a speech, I can make one, for I'm always thinkin' somethin', and thinkin' and talkin' is mighty near kin with me.' Says I, 'One thing I've been thinkin' is, that I'm like the old timber in the woods — long past my prime and ready to be cut down, and you all are the young trees strikin' your roots down and spreadin' your branches and askin' for room to grow in.' And says I, 'What I think about you ain't likely to be of much importance. I'm jest a plain, old-fashioned woman. The only sort o' club I ever belonged to was the Mite Society o' Goshen church, and the only service I ever did the State was

AUNT JANE GOES A-VISITING

raisin' a family o' sons and daughters, five sons and four daughters.' Says I, 'There's some folks that thinks women ought to do jest what their mothers and grandmothers did, but,' says I, 'every generation has its work. I've done mine and you're doin' yours. And,' says I, 'I look at you ladies sittin' here in your pretty parlors and your fine clothes, and back of every one of you I can see your grandmothers and your great-grandmothers, jest plain hard-workin' women like me. But,' says I, 'there ain't much difference between you, after all, except the difference in the clothes and the manners. Your grandmothers traveled their Wilderness Road, and you're travelin' yours, and one's as hard as the other. And,' says I, 'if I was in your place, I wouldn't pay a bit of attention to what the men folks said about me. Suppose you don't have as many children as your grandmothers had; I can tell by lookin' at your faces that you're good wives and good mothers; you love the three or four children you've got as well as your grandmothers loved their twelve or fifteen, and that's the main p'int — the way you love your children, not how many children you have. And further than that,' says I, 'there's such a thing nowadays as a woman havin' so many children that she hasn't got time to be a mother, but that's a p'int that men don't consider. And,' says I, ' when I think of all the good work you've done and all you're goin' to do, I feel like praisin' God. For I know you're helpin' this old world and this old State to go on like the apostle said we ought to go, " from glory to glory." '

"And bless your life," laughed Aunt Jane, " if they didn't clap their hands like they never would stop, and one lady come over and kissed me, and says, ' That's the best speech I ever heard at a woman's club.'

"And I reckon," concluded Aunt Jane with a gay laugh, " that if Uncle Billy happened to hear about me speakin' at a woman's club, he'd think that Sodom and Gomorrah was spreadin' clear down into the Goshen neighborhood."

"How would you like to live with Henrietta, Aunt Jane?" I asked.

"Child, child," said Aunt Jane with a reproving shake of her head, " you know better than to ask such a question. That visit to Henrietta's was like climbin' a hill that you've lived on the other side of all your life. I've been to the top o' the hill and seen what's on the other side, and I've come back to my own place,

AUNT JANE GOES A-VISITING

Solomon says there's a time for everything, and I don't need any Solomon to tell me that there's a place for everybody; and this old house and this old farm is the only place that could ever be home to me, and I'm here to stay till they carry me out through that gate yonder and lay my bones over in the old buryin'-ground alongside of Abram's and the children's and the rest of them that's gone before me."

V

THE MARRIAGE PROBLEM IN GOSHEN

V

THE MARRIAGE PROBLEM IN GOSHEN

AUNT JANE folded the country newspaper that she had been reading and laid it on the family Bible at her elbow. Her face was grave, and she sighed as she took up her knitting.

"I sometimes think, honey," she said, in answer to my look of inquiry, "that if I want to keep my faith in God and man I'll have to quit readin' the news-

THE LAND OF LONG AGO

papers. I try to believe that everything's goin' on all right with the world and that whatever happens is for the best, but I can't open a paper without readin' about some husband and wife that's parted from each other, and that looks like there's somethin' mighty wrong with this day and time. Me and Uncle Billy Bascom was talkin' about it last week, and Uncle Billy says, ' If folks'd only forsake their sins as easy as they forsake their husbands and their wives nowadays, this'd be a sanctified world.'

"No, child, the partin' of husbands and wives is one new-fangled way I can't git used to. Why, as far back as I can ricollect there never was but one woman in the Goshen neighborhood that left her husband, and that was Emmeline Amos, that married Henry Sanford. Emmeline was a first cousin to Sam Amos. Sam's father was Jeremiah Amos, and Emmeline's father was Middleton Amos. Emmeline was a pretty little thing, and sweet-tempered and smart about work, but her mother used to say that Emmeline had a mind like a piece o' changeable silk. She'd want a thing, and she wouldn't rest till she got it, and the minute she got it she'd fall out with it and want somethin' else. If she went to town and bought a blue dress, before she

MARRIAGE PROBLEM IN GOSHEN

got to the toll-gate she'd want to turn back and buy a pink one, and about the only thing she was constant in wantin' was Henry.

"They'd been sweethearts more or less all their lives, and it was a settled thing that they expected to be married as soon as Henry got his farm paid for. But before the day was set, the war broke out and Henry enlisted. It went mighty hard with him to leave Emmeline, but a man that stayed out o' the army for the sake of a gyirl didn't stand much chance with the gyirl or anybody else them days. Him and Emmeline wanted to be married before he went, but the old folks said no. Emmeline's mother says, 'This'll give Emmeline a chance to know her own mind and change it — if she's goin' to change it — before it's too late. If Henry comes back, well and good; and if he don't come back, it'll be all the better for Emmeline that she didn't marry him, for,' says she, 'a young gyirl's chances o' gittin' married are better than a widder's.'

"So Henry went, and Emmeline stayed and waited for him good and faithful. Towards the end of the war — I don't ricollect what battle it was — Henry got shot in the shoulder, and after stayin' some time in the hospittle he managed to come back home more dead than alive, and it was many a week before he was strong enough to be married. As soon as he was able to be up and walk around a little he begun to talk about marryin', and they said old lady Sanford took a lookin'-glass down from the wall and held it up before him and says she, ' Son, look at yourself. Do you think you can make a bridegroom out of a skeleton ? ' And says she, ' Son, there's jest two people in the world that wouldn't run from you if they saw you now, and one of 'em's your mother and the other's the undertaker.' Says she, ' Wait till you look like a human bein', and then it'll be time to set the weddin' day and bake the weddin' cake.'

"Well, finally, along in the fall, they got married, and settled down to housekeepin' as happy as you please. Emmeline was a mighty neat, orderly sort of a gyirl, and she went to work puttin' things to rights and makin' the house look homelike, and one mornin' she concluded she'd straighten out Henry's trunk. I've heard her tell about it many a time. She said Henry had his outside clothes all mixed up and his neckties and his socks scattered around all through the trunk, and she was foldin' things and stackin' 'em up together and singin' ' Flow Gently, Sweet Afton,' and all at once she

"'ONE MORNING SHE CONCLUDED SHE'D STRAIGHTEN
OUT HENRY'S TRUNK.'"
Page 148.

MARRIAGE PROBLEM IN GOSHEN

come across a little silk shirt. She said for a minute or so she couldn't take it in, and when she did, she dropped the shirt like it had been a rattlesnake, and she got so weak and faint she had to sit down on the side o' the bed. She said she didn't know how long she set there lookin' at the shirt and thinkin' terrible things about Henry and makin' up her mind what she'd say and do, when Henry come in from the field. She said she knew she ought to be cookin' dinner, and she went down in the kitchen and tried to, but to save her life she couldn't, her hands trembled so, and she couldn't keep her mind on what she was tryin' to do. So she went back up-stairs and set down by the trunk and waited. And when Henry come in and didn't see her in the kitchen and no signs of dinner anywhere, he come runnin' up-stairs to find her and started to put his arms around her and kiss her, but she pushed him off with both hands. And says he, 'Why, Emmeline, what on earth's the matter?' And she said she tried to answer him, but her voice wouldn't come, and she jest p'inted to the shirt lyin' on the floor.

"At first Henry didn't understand; but he looked at the shirt and he looked at her face, and then he burst out laughin', and says he, 'Well, that does look pretty bad, sure enough; but I know you've got too much confidence in me to let a little thing like that worry you'; and he tried to take hold of her hand, but she jerked it away, and by that time she was so mad at him for laughin' at her that she didn't find any trouble about talkin', and the madder she got and the more she talked, the harder Henry laughed, and says he: 'Oh! come now, Emmeline. You mustn't be so hard on a man. I never loved that woman like I love you. I never was married to her, and I never wanted to marry her. Ain't that enough to satisfy you?'

"Emmeline said she didn't know she could feel so wicked; but when Henry said that, she felt as if she wanted to kill somebody — she didn't know whether it was Henry or the other woman — and she jumped up and run out o' the room, slammin' the door behind her as hard as she could, and locked herself in the spare bedroom. She said Henry went down-stairs, and she could hear him goin' around in the kitchen and pantry lookin' for cold meat and bread, and she looked out o' the window and watched till she saw him go back to the field. And the minute he was out o' sight, she packed her trunk and went to the stable and saddled the mare her father had made her a present of when

MARRIAGE PROBLEM IN GOSHEN

she married, and then she dressed herself and wrote a note sayin' she'd gone back to her father's house and she'd send over for her trunk the next day. She pinned the note to Henry's piller, and then she got on her horse and started for home.

"Old man Middleton was sittin' on the front porch smokin' his pipe when Emmeline rode up, and he hollered out to his wife that here was Emmeline, and they both come runnin' out to meet her. You know how it is with the old folks, when a gyirl comes home to make 'em a visit after gittin' married. They're proud of her for marryin' well, but they've been missin' her and they're mighty glad to have her back in her old place. But as soon as they'd hugged her and kissed her they both said, 'Where's Henry?' and, 'Why didn't he come with you?' Emmeline said for a minute she wished she was back at home, for she knew how bad they'd feel when she told 'em what she had to tell. But she thought she might as well have it over and be done with it, and says she, 'Henry's at home, and I'm at home, too. I've left him, and I'm never goin' back to him.'

"Well, Emmeline said they both fell back on the porch steps like they'd been shot, and as soon as they could speak they both said: 'Left him! What for?' Emmeline said she felt so ashamed of Henry she'd made up her mind from the first that nobody ever should know about that little silk shirt. So she says, 'I've found out that Henry's not the man I thought he was. I've left him for good and all.' And old man Middleton says, 'Why, daughter, what's he done amiss? I've known Henry from a boy up, and there ain't a man in the county I'd rather have for a son-in-law.' And Emmeline says, 'Yes, I used to think that way myself, but I've found out different.' And the old man says, 'Has he struck you or mistreated you in any way? He's been too well brought up for that. He ain't close-fisted about money matters, I know, for I've had dealin's with him myself, and, besides, you ain't been married to him long enough to have to call on him for anything.' And Emmeline says, 'No, he's as freehanded as he can be, and I've got nothin' to complain about except that I didn't know him as well as I do now, and since I know him, why, I don't want to live with him.'

"And then her mother begun questionin', and all she could git out of Emmeline was that Henry wasn't the man she thought he was; and at last the old lady

MARRIAGE PROBLEM IN GOSHEN

lost her patience and says she, 'In the name o' peace! Have I got a child with so little sense as to think that that's any reason for leavin' a man? Of course he ain't the man you thought he was, and you ain't the woman he thought you was. But what o' that? If husbands and wives took to partin' on that account, the world would be full o' grass-widders and grass-widderers.' Says she, 'You're welcome to stay here till Henry comes for you, and I'll give out to the neighbors that you're makin' us a visit, but back to Henry you've got to go. Gittin' married,' says she, 'is like buyin' a piece o' dress-goods at the store. As long as you haven't had it cut off the bolt, you can change your mind, but if it's once cut off, you've got to pay for it and take it home and make the best o' your bargain.' Says she, 'You had plenty o' time to find out what sort o' man Henry was, and you turned your back on two good chances whilst you waited for him, and now there's no slippin' out o' the trade. I don't propose to have any widders in my family,' says she, 'except the sort that can put up a tombstone and wear a black veil.' Says she, 'Take off your bonnet and make yourself at home till Henry comes for you.'

"And, bless your life, Henry wasn't long comin',

either. Before they got the supper dishes washed up, here he come as fast as his horse could bring him. Old man Amos went out to meet him and took him around to the side o' the house and says he, ' Son, I want you to tell me what all this to-do is, anyhow. I can't git head nor tail of it from Emmeline.' And Henry says, ' Well, Father Amos, it's this way. Emmeline's been goin' through my trunk, and she found a little somethin' or other that belonged to another woman that I used to know long before I knew her, and that's what upset her.' And the old man shook his head and says he, ' You ought to 'a' destroyed all such things before you married; and that was a mighty keerless trick, leavin' your trunk unlocked, though two to one Emmeline would 'a' got into it anyway. It's my belief,' says he, ' that women carry skeleton keys to keep the run o' their husband's private affairs.' And Henry says, ' I've done all I could to pacify her; I've told her I never loved that woman like I love her and never was married to the woman and never wanted to marry her, and what more can a man say ? ' And the old man says, ' Well, that ought to satisfy any reasonable woman, but in matters like this women don't seem to be able to use their reason.' Says he, ' It looks like they expect

MARRIAGE PROBLEM IN GOSHEN

a man to be jest like Adam before Eve was made for him,' and says he, 'You'll have to hoe your own row with Emmeline in this affair, and her mother and me'll help you all we can.'

"Well, all three of 'em argued with Emmeline, tryin' to persuade her to go back home, but nothin' they could say had any effect on her. And finally Henry says, 'Well, Emmeline, if you will leave me, I reckon I'll have to put up with it, but I've got jest one favor to ask of you.' Says he, 'You know how my mother and father have set their hearts on havin' you for a daughter-in-law and how anxious they are to see you. Now, all I ask of you is to let me take you to see my folks, and you make 'em a visit. If I was to write to my mother,' says he, 'that my wife had left me, I believe it would be the death of her. She's subject to spells anyway, and the doctor says any little shock'll carry her off. So you let me take you up to mother's, and you make her and father a little visit, and then I'll bring you home and try to break it to mother the best I can.'

"Emmeline thought a minute, and finally she says, 'Well, I'll go for your mother's sake, but not for yours.' So Henry, he went back home to git somebody to look

THE LAND OF LONG AGO

after his stock while he was gone, and the next day he come for Emmeline, and they started to his mother's. It was pretty near a day's journey, and there couldn't 'a' been a nicer trip for a bride and groom, ridin' through the woods and over the hills about the middle of October, the leaves jest turnin' and the weather neither hot nor cold. I reckon, child, you don't know what it is to make a journey that way. That's one o' the things folks miss by bein' born nowadays instead of in the old times before there was any railroads. I ricollect when they begun puttin' down the track for the first railroad in this county. Uncle Jimmy Judson went to town on purpose to see what it was like, and some o' the town folks explained all about layin' the ties and the rails and showed him a picture o' the cyars and the locomotive, and Uncle Jimmy looked at it a minute or two, and then he shook his head and says he, 'None o' that sort o' travelin' for me — shut up in a wooden box with a steam-engine in front liable to blow up any minute, and nothin' but the mercy o' God to keep them wheels from runnin' off this here narrer railin'.' Says he, 'Give me a clear sky overhead, a good road underfoot, good company by my side, and my old buggy and my old mare, and I can travel from sunup to sundown and ask no odds o' the railroad.' And I reckon most old people feel pretty much like Uncle Jimmy.

"I ricollect Parson Page sayin' once that the Christian's life was a journey to heaven, and Sam Amos says, 'Yes, and generally when I start out to go to a place, I want to get there as soon as possible; but here's one time,' says he, 'when I wouldn't care if I never got to my journey's end.' And that's the way it was with me when me and Abram'd start out in our old rockaway for a day's travel through the country, goin' to see his mother or mine. No matter how much I wanted to see the folks I was goin' to, I'd feel as if I could keep on forever ridin' through the thick woods or along the open road, the wind blowin' in my face and the sun gittin' higher and higher towards noon and then night comin' on before we'd be at our journey's end.

"I've heard Emmeline laugh many a time about that ride. Her mother come out to the gate and put a basket o' lunch under the seat, and says she, 'Now, Emmeline, you be a good gyirl and don't give Henry any more trouble, and, Henry, when you two come back you take Emmeline right home with you; don't you bring her here.' And old man Amos give a big laugh and says

THE LAND OF LONG AGO

he, ' Come back home if you want to, Emmeline. My door's always open to my own children; but if you come, Henry's got to come, too, so either way you fix it there won't be any partin'.' Emmeline said she wouldn't let Henry help her in the buggy. She got in on one side, and he got in on the other, and she set as far off from him as she could, and they started off, old lady Amos callin' after 'em: ' You jest remember, Emmeline, as long as Henry's above the sod you're Henry's wife. There's only one thing that can part you, and that's death.'

" Well, Emmeline said Henry was as nice and polite as you please all that day. He talked about the weather and the birds and the trees and the flowers, and p'inted out things along the way, but she never opened her mouth till dinner-time. They stopped by a spring to eat their dinner, and Henry watered the horse and fixed the check-rein so's he could graze, and then he set down some little distance away from her, and she opened the basket. She said of course she couldn't be mean enough to sit there and eat by herself, so she told him to come and have some dinner. And he come over and set down beside her, and she waited on him, and they drank out o' the same cup, and Emmeline

MARRIAGE PROBLEM IN GOSHEN

said you could hear the spring drippin' and the birds and the squirrels chirpin' and chatterin' in the trees; and every now and then a pretty leaf'd come flutterin' down and fall in the spring or on her lap, and Henry talked so kind and pleasant that Emmeline said she got to thinkin' how happy she'd be if it wasn't for that little silk shirt, and she'd 'a' give anything she had if she'd jest kept out o' Henry's trunk. And when they'd got through eatin', Henry took hold of her hand and says he, ' Emmeline, can't you trust me a little bit ? ' And she jerked away from him and begun getherin' up the provisions and foldin' the napkins. And Henry says, ' Well, pretty soon we'll be at mother's. Maybe she can set matters right.' And they got in the buggy and started again, and Emmeline said the nearer they got to Henry's home the worse she felt, and finally she broke down and begun to cry, and she cried for three miles right straight along.

"It was about sunset, and Henry kept tellin' her to cheer up and look at the pretty clouds and the light comin' through the red-and-yeller sugar-maples and the beech-trees. She said he was mighty cheerful himself, and it made her mad to see how easy he was takin' it. When they got within sight o' the house Henry

THE LAND OF LONG AGO

says, 'Now dry your eyes, Emmeline, or mother'll think you ain't glad to see her. She goin' to be mighty glad to see you.' Old man Sanford and his wife, honey, was a couple that thought more o' their daughters-in-law than they did o' their own children. They'd had nine sons and never had a gyirl-child, and they'd always wanted one, and the old man used to look at the boys and say, 'Well, your mother and me didn't want this many boys, but you children would be boys, and now you've got to make up for the disapp'intment you've been to your parents by bringin' us in some nice, pretty daughters-in-law.' And every time one o' the boys got married the old man, he'd say, 'Well, my daughters are comin' at last,' and the old lady used to say that her daughters-in-law paid her for all the trouble her sons had been to her.

"It was milkin'-time when they drove in at the big gate, and the old lady was jest startin' out with her quart cup and her bucket. Henry hollered, 'Howdy, mother!' and she dropped the milk things and run to meet 'em, and Emmeline said she never had such a welcome in her life. The old lady didn't take any notice o' Henry. She jest hugged and kissed Emmeline and pretty near carried her into the house. Then she

MARRIAGE PROBLEM IN GOSHEN

took notice of how Emmeline had been cryin', and she turned around to Henry and says she, 'Henry Sanford, what have you been doin' to this poor child to make her cry? It speaks mighty poorly of you to have your wife cryin' this soon in your married life.' And Henry put his hand in his coat pocket and pulled out a little bundle and handed it to his mother and says he, 'Mother, I want you to tell Emmeline whose this is.' And the old lady opened the bundle and says she, 'Henry Sanford, what do you mean by pokin' this old shirt at me when I want to be makin' the acquaintance o' my new daughter-in-law?' And Henry says, 'If you'll tell Emmeline all about this shirt, mother, it'll stop her cryin'.' Emmeline said the old lady put on her specs and looked at 'em both as if she thought they might be losin' their senses and says she, 'Well, honey, I don't see what this old shirt has to do with your cryin', but I can mighty soon tell you about it. It's one of a half a dozen that Henry's father didn't have any better sense than to buy five or six years ago when he was layin' in a stock o' summer goods. (" Old man Sanford run a country store, child, along with his farmin'," interpolated Aunt Jane.) And,' says she, 'after they'd stayed in the store three or four seasons

I took 'em and wore 'em to keep 'em from bein' a dead loss. And when Henry come out o' the army he was half naked and more'n half dead, betwixt the Yankees and the chills and fever, and I put these shirts on him to protect his chest.'

"Well, Emmeline said as soon as the old lady begun talkin', her heart got as light as a feather, and she felt like a thousand pounds had been lifted off of her mind. But she said she looked around at Henry, and he was watchin' to see how she'd take it, and all at once he burst out laughin', and that made her mad again, and she thought about all the trouble she'd been through, and she begun cryin' again and says she, 'Oh! why didn't you tell me that? Why didn't you tell me?' Emmeline said Henry's mother come over and put her arms around her and says she, 'Henry Sanford, what prank have you been playin' on your wife? Tell me this minute.' And Henry begun explainin' things and tryin' to smooth it over, and I reckon he thought his mother'd see the joke jest like he did, but she didn't. She looked at Henry over her spectacles mighty stern and says she, 'Henry, I've always been afeard you didn't have your full share o' punishment whilst you were growin' up, bein' the youngest child, and if it

MARRIAGE PROBLEM IN GOSHEN

wasn't that you're a married man I'd certainly give you one o' the whippin's you missed when you were a boy.' And Henry says, ' Well, maybe I ought to be punished for not tellin' Emmeline, but I jest thought I'd play a joke on her, and if Emmeline had only had a little confidence in me it wouldn't 'a' worried her the way it did.' And old lady Sanford, she says, ' Confidence! Confidence! There's jest one person I put my confidence in, and that's Almighty God.' Says she, ' If a man's crippled in both feet, and the front door and the back door's locked, and I've got both my eyes on him, I may make out to trust him a minute or two, but that's about all.' Says she, ' Of course a woman ought to trust her husband; but that don't mean that she's got to shut her eyes and her ears and throw away her common sense.' Says she, ' Emmeline don't know as much about you as your father knows about that old roan mare he bought day before yesterday. A man's jest like a horse,' says she; ' you've got to break him in and learn all his gaits and tricks before there's any safety or pleasure travelin' with him. Here you ain't been married to Emmeline a month yet, and you talk about her havin' confidence in you!' Says she, ' I've been married to your father forty-five years this comin' January, and I've never seen cause to doubt him, but if I was to find another woman's gyarment amongst his clothes I'd leave him that quick.'

"And about this time old man Sanford come in, and when he'd shook hands with Henry and hugged and kissed Emmeline he begun to take notice of how she'd been cryin', and the old lady she told him the whole story, and, bless your life, the old man was madder'n she was. He turned around to Henry and says he, mighty stern and solemn, 'Son, I feel that you've disgraced your raisin'.' Says he, 'A man that'll cause a woman to shed an unnecessary tear is worse'n a brute, and here you've let Emmeline cry her pretty eyes out over nothin' right at the beginnin' of her married life. If you treat her this way now, how'll it be ten years from now?' And then he patted Emmeline on the shoulder and says he, 'Never mind, daughter, if Henry don't treat you right, you stay here with pappy and mammy and be their little gyirl. Henry always was the black sheep o' the flock, anyhow.'

"And at that Emmeline jumped up and run over to Henry and threw her arms around his neck and says she, 'You sha'n't talk that way about Henry. He's not a black sheep, either. He's the best man in the

MARRIAGE PROBLEM IN GOSHEN

world, and it's all my fault and I'll never mistrust him again as long as I live.' And then Henry broke down and cried, and the old man and the old lady they cried, and they all hugged and kissed each other, and such a makin' up you never did see. And in two or three days here Henry and Emmeline come ridin' back home and lookin' like a sure-enough bride and groom. Emmeline said they went over the same road, but everything seemed different; the birds sung sweeter, the sun shone brighter, and the leaves were prettier, for you know, honey, the way a thing looks depends more on people's minds than it does on their eyes. They stopped at the same spring to eat their dinner, and Emmeline said she promised Henry she'd never mistrust him again, and he promised her he'd never play any more jokes on her. I reckon they both must 'a' kept their promise, for from that time on there never was a more peaceable, well-contented married couple than Emmeline and Henry. Emmeline used to say that she did all her cryin' durin' her honeymoon and Henry'd never caused her to shed a tear since.

"Nobody ever would 'a' known about her findin' the shirt and leavin' her husband if she hadn't told it herself, for the old folks on both sides felt so ashamed o' Henry and Emmeline for the way they'd acted that they never would 'a' told it. But Emmeline told Milly Amos and Milly told Sam, and the first thing you knew everybody in Goshen was laughin' over Emmeline leavin' her husband, and everybody was disputin' about which was in the right and which was in the wrong. I ricollect Sam Amos sayin' that any woman that went rummagin' around in a man's trunk deserved to find trouble, and his sympathies was all with Henry; and Milly said Henry ought to 'a' told Emmeline whose shirt it was and not kept her grievin' and worryin' all that time. And Sam says, ' Yes, he ought to 'a' told her, but if he had 'a' told her it wouldn't 'a' helped matters, for she wasn't in a frame o' mind to believe him.' Says he, ' You women are always suspicionin' a man, and if you come across a piece of circumstantial evidence you'll convict him on that and hang him in spite of all he can say for himself.'

"I ricollect our Mite Society got to talkin' one day about husbands and wives leavin' each other, and whether it was ever right or lawful for married folks to part and marry again. Maria Petty says, says she, ' There's some things that every woman's called on to stand, and there's some things that no woman ought

MARRIAGE PROBLEM IN GOSHEN

to stand.' And Sally Ann says, 'Yes, and as long as you women think you have to stand things, you'll have things to stand.' And Milly Amos says, 'A husband and a wife can part when there's no children, but,' says she, 'if they've had children, you might put the husband on one side o' the world and the wife on the other and they're husband and wife still, for there's the children holdin' 'em together.' I ricollect everybody had a different opinion, and the longer we talked the further we got from any sort of agreement about it."

And as it was in Goshen so was it in Athens when Plato wrote and taught, and so it is to-day wherever human wisdom offers its varying solutions to this problem of the ages.

"What do you think about it, Aunt Jane?" I asked.

Aunt Jane was silent. Intuitively she felt the magnitude of the question. We had laughed over the comedy of her story, but its rustic scenery had shifted, and we were standing now in the tragic presence of a social sphinx whose mystery calls for baffled silence rather than confident speech.

"Well, honey," she said at last, thoughtfully and hesitatingly, "if folks could only love each other the way me and Abram did, they'll never want to part; and of course if they love each other they'll trust each other; and if the love and the trust runs short, why, then they ought to be patient and try to bear with each other's failin's. But, as Maria Petty used to say, there's some things that no woman is called on to bear, and no man, either, for that matter, and if married folks feel that they can't stand livin' together I ain't the one to judge 'em, for I never had anything to stand, and happy folks oughtn't to judge the folks that's unhappy. It does look like to me that if the husbands and wives in Goshen could stay married anybody could, but maybe I don't know. And when a person gits all twisted and turned so's they can't tell what's right and what's wrong, why, it ain't time for passin' judgment and givin' opinions, and I reckon I'll jest have to fall back on that text o' Scripture that says all things are workin' together for good. Not some things, honey, but 'all things.' Did you ever think o' that? The things you want and the things you don't want; the things you complain about and the things you rejoice about; the things you laugh over and the things you cry over — all of 'em workin', not against each other, but together, and all workin' for good. I ricollect

MARRIAGE PROBLEM IN GOSHEN

hearin' a sermon once on that very passage o' Scripture. The preacher said that that text was like a sea without a shore; its meanin' was as wide and as deep as the love of God, and if we could only take it in and believe it, we'd never have any fears or any misgivin's again. And then, there's that verse o' Brownin's that says God's in his heaven and everything's right with the world. So I reckon, in spite of all this marryin' and partin' and marryin' again, the world's in safe hands and movin' on in the right way."

Aunt Jane was smiling now, for on these winged words of apostle and poet her soul had risen into its native atmosphere of serene faith, casting upon the shoulders of Omnipotence the burden of world-sorrow and world-sin that only Omnipotence can lift and bear.

VI
AN EYE FOR AN EYE

VI

AN EYE FOR AN EYE

IT was the time of the blooming of the wistaria. Over in fair Japan the imperial purple clusters were drooping over the roofs of the tea-gardens and the walls of the Emperor's palace, and here in Aunt Jane's garden they hung from the rickety trellis that barely supported the weight of the royal flowers.

Aunt Jane gazed at them with worshipful eyes.

"It's been fifty years this spring," she said, "since

THE LAND OF LONG AGO

I planted that vine. It took it five years to come into bloomin', so I've seen it bloom forty-five times; and every time I see it, it looks prettier to me. I took a root of it along with me when I went to Lexin'ton to visit Henrietta, and the gyardener planted it by the front porch so's it could run up the big pillars — that's the difference betwixt my gyarden and Henrietta's. She has a gyardener to plant her flowers, and I do my own plantin'. I can't help believin' that I have more pleasure out o' my old-fashioned gyarden than she has out o' her fine new one. Flowers that somebody else plants and 'tends to are jest like children that somebody else nurses and raises. I raise my flowers like I raised my children, and I reckon that that's why I love 'em so. It's a curious thing, child, the hold that flowers and trees has on human bein's. You can move into a house and set up your furniture and live there twenty years, and as long as you don't do any plantin', you won't mind changin' your house any more'n you'd mind changin' your dress. But you jest plant a rose-bush or a honey-suckle and then start to move, and it'll look like every root o' that bush is holdin' you to the place, and if you go, you'll want to take your flowers with you jest like grand-

"IT WAS THE TIME OF THE BLOOMING OF THE WISTARIA."
Page 173.

AN EYE FOR AN EYE

mother took her rose when she moved from old Virginia to new Kentucky."

She paused to look again at the splendor of grace and color that spring had brought to the old garden. No wonder we have patience to tread the ice-bound path through the winter when we know that things like this lie at the end. A delicate, reverent wind arose, the long, rich tassels of bloom yielded themselves to its touch and swayed to and fro like majesty acknowledging homage, while, bolder than the wind, a mob of democratic bees hummed nonchalantly in the august presence and gathered honey as if a wistaria were no more than a country clover field.

"Henrietta was tellin' me," continued Aunt Jane, "that over yonder in Japan when the cherry trees and this vine blooms, everybody takes a holiday and turns out and enjoys the flowers and the sunshine, and I says to Henrietta, 'That's no new thing to me, honey, I've been doin' that all my life.' I like housekeepin' as well as anybody, but when spring comes and the flowers begin bloomin', a house can't hold me. There's one time o' the year about the middle o' May, when it's all I can do to keep myself inside the house long enough to do the cookin' and wash the dishes. I ricollect the first spring after I was married there was one day when Abram said that he had bread and butter and pinks for breakfast, and bread and butter and roses for dinner, and bread and butter and honeysuckles for supper. You know the Bible says, ' Let your moderation be known unto all men,' and I always tried to be moderate about housekeepin'. Sam Amos used to say that women kept house for two reasons: one was to please themselves and the other was to displease the men. Says he, ' The Bible says we come from the dirt and we're goin' back to the dirt, so why can't we live in the dirt and say nothin' about it?' Says he, ' Give me three meals a day and a comfortable place to sleep in, and let me be able to lay my hands on my clothes when I want 'em, and that's housekeepin' enough for me.' I reckon most men's pretty much like Sam; and seein' how little a man cares about havin' a house kept, it looks like it's foolish for women to spend so much o' their time sweepin' and keepin' things in order. Mother used to think I took housekeepin' too easy. I ricollect once she was spendin' the day with me and I let a dish fall, a mighty pretty china bowl with pink roses on it, and she begun sayin' what a pity it was, and

AN EYE FOR AN EYE

how keerless I must 'a' been to let it slip out o' my hands, and I jest laughed and picked up the pieces and says I, 'Dishes and promises are made to break. There's a time app'inted for every dish to break, jest as there is for every person to die, and this bowl's time had come.' And Mother, she laughed, and says she, 'Well, Jane, you'll never die of the housekeepin' disease.' And I wouldn't be surprised, child, if my gyardenin' and my easy goin' ways wasn't the reason why I'm here to-day watchin' my flowers grow instead o' bein' out yonder in the old buryin' ground with Hannah Crawford and the rest o' the Goshen women. Hannah took her housekeepin' like Amos Matthews took his religion, and that was what broke her down and carried her off before her time."

Clouds were floating across the sun and a delicate shadow lay over the flower-beds around us. Aunt Jane's eyes were on the distant hills beyond the budding orchard trees, and I saw with delight that she was in the garden but not of it. A few moments ago the present beauty of the wistaria had possessed her, but now she was living in another spring.

"Dr. Pendleton used to tell Hannah that her name ought to 'a' been Martha, because she was troubled about many things," continued Aunt Jane; " and it was her takin' trouble over things that come near throwin' her off her balance, back yonder in '54, the year we had the big drouth. Maybe you've heard your grandmother tell about it, child. Parson Page used to say there was nothin' like a drouth for makin' people feel their dependence on a higher power, and I reckon more prayers went up to heaven that summer than'd gone up for many a year, and folks prayed then that never had prayed before. A time like that is mighty hard on man and beast. The heavens were brass and the earth cast iron jest like the Bible says. Every livin' thing was parched up and I ricollect Sam Amos sayin' that, with the cistern and the spring dry and the river a mile and a half away, for once in his life he found it easier to be godly than to be clean.

" Well, about the time when everything was at its worst, we had a strange preacher to fill the pulpit o' Goshen church, and he preached a sermon that none of us ever forgot. There's two kinds of preachers, child, the New Testament preachers and the Old Testament preachers. Parson Page was the New Testament kind. Sam Amos used to say that Parson Page's sermons never interfered with

AN EYE FOR AN EYE

anybody's Sunday evenin' nap. But the minute I laid eyes on the new preacher, I says to myself, 'We're goin' to have an Old Testament sermon, this day,' and sure enough we did. He was a tall, thin man, with the blackest eyes and hair you ever saw and a mouth that looked like he'd never smiled in his life, and when he walked up into the pulpit you'd 'a' thought he was one o' the old prophets come to warn men of judgment to come. He read the twenty-first chapter of Exodus, that chapter that's all about judgments and punishments; and then he turned over to Leviticus and read a chapter there about the same things, and then he picked out two texts from these chapters. One was, 'Thou shalt give life for life, eye for eye, tooth for tooth, hand for hand, foot for foot, burning for burning, wound for wound, stripe for stripe.' And the other one was, 'And if a man cause a blemish in his neighbor, as he hath done, so shall it be done to him. Breach for breach, eye for eye, tooth for tooth.'

"Well, honey, the sermon he preached from them two texts was somethin' terrible. He begun by sayin' that the kingdom of God was a kingdom of justice; that every sin brought its own punishment with it, and there was no escapin' it. He said God had fixed the penalty for every sin committed by every sinner; we couldn't always tell what the punishment would be, one sinner would be punished one way and another sinner another way, and one would have his punishment right at once, and the other might not have his for a good many years, but it was sure to come at last. He never said a word about the blood of Christ, and the only time he brought up the New Testament was when he told about Christ sayin' that we had to pay the uttermost farthing.

"Now, of course, child, all o' this is in the Bible, and it must be true. But then, there's other texts that's jest as true and a heap more comfortin', and if Parson Page had been preachin' that day, he'd 'a' taken a text about forgiveness and atonement, but maybe we wouldn't 'a' remembered that as long as we remembered the other preacher's sermon. I ricollect when meetin' broke everybody appeared to be laborin' under a sense o' sin, and instead o' shakin' hands and talkin' awhile as we generally did, we all went home as quick as we could. Uncle Jim Mathews said it took him a week to git over the effects o' that sermon, and Sam Amos says, 'I thought I was doin'

AN EYE FOR AN EYE

right in lettin' that shiftless tenant o' mine off from payin' his year's rent, I felt so sorry for his wife and children; but,' says he, ' in strict justice and accordin' to this " eye for an eye " doctrine, I ought to hold him to his contract and make him pay.'

"Well, it wasn't long after this till we begun to hear curious tales about the Crawford farm. Abram come in one day and says he, ' Jane, I never have believed in ghosts and spirits, but upon my soul,' says he, ' Miles Crawford's been tellin' me some things that make me think maybe there's such a thing after all.' And he went on to tell how Miles had had his straw stacks pulled down, and the fodder scattered all over the barn floor, and his tools carried off and hid in fence corners, and his bags o' seed spilled around, and he couldn't tell when it was done nor who did it. Of course the talk spread all over the neighborhood, and every week there'd be some new happenin', till folks begun to say the place was ha'nted and nobody liked to pass it after dark.

"Well, one day about the last day of August Abram went to town on some business or other, and I went with him. I ricollect the drouth had broke, and the grass and flowers and trees buddin' out made it look jest like spring. Well, we went joggin' along the pike, laughin' and talkin', and as we passed Miles Crawford's place we saw Miles come out on the front porch and look up and down the road. When he saw us, he come runnin' down the path and motioned to us to stop, and when he got within speakin' distance he called out, 'If you're goin' to town, stop by Dr. Pendleton's and tell him to come out here as quick as he can, for Hannah's lost her senses.' Says he, 'She's been at the bottom of all the devilment that's been done on the farm for the last month, and this mornin',' says he, 'I set a watch and caught her at it, and she's crazy as a loon.' With that I jumped out o' the buggy, and says I, 'Drive on, Abram, I'm goin' to stay with Hannah till the doctor comes.' So Abram drove off, and I went on to the house with Miles. He was mighty excited and put out, and kept talkin' about the trouble he'd had and blamin' Hannah for it. And Hannah was rockin' herself back and forth, laughin' and cryin' and sayin', 'An eye for an eye and a tooth for a tooth.' I saw in a minute she was in a mighty bad fix, and I was jest wonderin' what on earth I would do till the doctor got there, and I put up a prayer that Abram wouldn't be long findin' him; but that very minute

AN EYE FOR AN EYE

I heard the sound of two buggies on the pike. Abram had met the doctor comin' out to Goshen, and turned around and come back with him, and the minute I saw the doctor's old broad-brimmed hat, I says to myself, 'It's all right now.' I don't reckon there ever was a man that understood women like the old doctor did, and him an old bachelor at that. I used to think it was a pity he hadn't married; he'd 'a' made such a good, kind husband. But then, bein' the man he was, he couldn't marry."

There was both paradox and enigma in this statement, and I asked for an explanation.

"Now, child," said Aunt Jane, "you're throwin' me clear off the track. For pity's sake let me get through with one story before you start me on another. As I was sayin', the old doctor come; but with Miles ragin' around and threatenin' to send Hannah to the Asylum, and Hannah cryin' and laughin' and sayin', 'An eye for an eye and a tooth for a tooth,' and me tryin' to pacify Hannah and Abram tryin' to pacify Miles, it was some time before he could come to an understandin' of the case; and when he begun to see daylight he turned around to Miles as stern as if he was reprovin' a child, and says he, 'Not another word,

Miles! If you can't hold your tongue go out of the room, for every time you speak you're makin' Hannah that much worse.' And he turns around to me and says he, 'Have you any idea what Hannah means by saying "An eye for an eye and a tooth for a tooth?"' And I says, 'Doctor, do you ricollect the sermon that strange minister preached about a month ago?' Says I, 'I may be wrong, but it's my belief that that sermon helped to put Hannah in the fix she's in now.' And the doctor, he thought a minute, and then he nodded his head right slow, and says he, 'I remember that sermon. It was not a wholesome sort of a discourse for any one to listen to.' Says he, 'It might not hurt a healthy person, but if there was anyone in the congregation with a sick mind, such a person couldn't be benefited by it.' And then he says to Hannah, 'Was it that sermon that put it into your head to tear down Miles's corn shocks?' And Hannah laughed and wrung her hands together and rocked herself backward and forward, and says she, 'Yes, that was it. Miles has been undoin' my work and givin' me trouble for thirty-five years, and I've wished many a time I could pay him back and make him see how hard it was, but I couldn't bring myself to do

AN EYE FOR AN EYE

what I wanted to do till I heard that sermon. I found out then that God wanted me to pay Miles back, and I'm glad I pulled his corn shocks to pieces, and tore down the straw stacks and scattered the bran all over the stable floor. May be he knows now how hard I have to work to keep house for him, and may be he'll be more keerful about litterin' the house up and pullin' things to pieces.' Says she, ' I work from mornin' till night, but there's always somethin' left undone. Before I get through with the breakfast dishes and cleanin' the house and churnin', it's time to cook dinner, and by the time I've cooked dinner and cleaned up the dishes and sewed and mended a little, it's time to cook supper and attend to the milkin', and I try to see after the children, but there's always somethin' undone.' Says she, ' I believe I could ketch up with my work, if Miles would only stop undoin' what I do. But it looks like I can't keep up any longer,' says she, ' with him workin' against me all the time.' And Miles says, ' You hear that? You hear that? Talkin' about lookin' after the children, and every child grown and married and gone long ago! She's crazy, crazy as a loon!' The doctor turned around and give Miles a look that hushed him up. And then he took hold of Hannah's hand and smoothed it right gentle and easy, and says he, 'That's right, tell me all your troubles; a trouble is easier to bear after you've told it to somebody.'

"It looked like Hannah's tongue was loosed, and she went on talkin' harder and faster than I ever had known her to talk before. Says she, 'I never was a lazy woman, and I always kept up with my work, I always loved to work, and Miles never could say I slighted anything about the house, but now it's different. It looks like there's a change come over me. I can't do what I used to do, and there's times when I don't seem to keer how things go. I reckon it's my fault, and I'm always blamin' myself for not gittin' more done, but I can't help it. There's a change come over me, and I ain't the woman I was a year ago.'

"The doctor, he was listenin' to it all jest as kind and earnest as you please, and he nodded his head and says, 'Yes, I understand it all, and I know exactly how you feel.' And he put his fingers on Hannah's wrist and thought a minute, and says he, 'Hannah, my child,' — No matter how old a woman was, honey," said Aunt Jane, interrupting herself, "Dr. Pendleton would always say 'my child' or 'my

AN EYE FOR AN EYE

daughter,' or ' my sister ' when he was talkin' to her. Maria Petty used to say that jest the sound of his voice was as good as medicine to a sick person. And says he, ' There's one more question I want to ask you: Is there anything you can think of that you'd like to have or like to do? '

"And Hannah put her hand up to her face and burst out cryin' like a little child, and the old doctor patted her on the shoulder and says he, ' That's right; cry as much as you please,' and when Hannah had kind o' quieted down, he says again, ' Now tell me what it is you want; I know there's somethin' you want, and if you can get it, it'll make you well.' And Hannah begun cryin' again, and says she, ' If I told you what it is I want, you'd think I'm crazy sure enough, and may be I am. My head feels heavy and dizzy,' says she, ' and sometimes I feel like I was goin' to fall backward, and I can't remember things like I used to do; I don't take any interest in my work, and I can't git to sleep at night for a long time, and I wake up at two o'clock and stay awake till daylight, and jest as I'm droppin' off, it's time to git up and cook breakfast, and I'm so tired that sometimes I wish the end of the world would come and put a stop to everything. But I don't want to go to the Asylum. Don't let Miles send me there.' And the doctor says, ' Don't you be afraid of that. Miles will never send you to an asylum while I'm alive to protect you. But you must tell me what it is you want. There's some little thing,' says he, ' that'll make you well, and you know what it is better than I do.' Well, Hannah held back like a child that's afraid of a whippin', but finally she says, ' You know that pasture at the back o' the house. I can see it from the kitchen window. Miles sowed it in clover last year, and the clover's come up since the rain and it's bloomin' now, and there's two or three big oak trees in the middle o' the field and the cows come up and lie down in the shade o' the trees; and every time I look out o' the window while I'm washin' dishes and makin' up bread, I think if I could jest lie down in the shade of the trees and look up at the sky all day and know there was somebody up here in the kitchen doin' my work, I'd get well and strong again.' And the doctor's eyes filled up with tears, and he patted Hannah on the back and says he, ' Poor child! Poor child! ' And then he turned around to Miles, and says he, ' Miles, do you hear that? There's nothing in the world the matter with Hannah, except that she's worked to death.' Says he, 'Go down to that pasture at once and turn the cows into some other field. Hannah shall have her wish before I leave this house.' Miles was an older man than the doctor, honey, but he minded the same as if he'd been his son; and while he was turnin' the cows out, we got some old comforts and a piller, and all of us went down to the pasture and spread the quilt under the tree. The doctor made Hannah lay down, and says he, 'Now, shut your eyes and let the sun and the wind take care of you. They're the best nurses in the world;' and says he, 'I'll drop by again in an hour or so to see how you're getting on, and Miles will come down every little while to bring you a glass of water and something to eat. You must stay here until the sun goes down, and then come up to the house and go right to bed.'

" So we all walked back to the house, and the doctor went to the front room where he'd left his medicine case, and he picked it up and turned around and faced Miles, and says he, 'Miles, lose no time about getting some one to do your work, for Hannah's going to rest under that tree for many a day.' Says he, 'There's a time in a woman's life when every burden ought to be lifted from her shoulders, and Hannah's reached that time. She's like a worn out field that's borne its harvests year after year and needs to lie fallow for awhile.' Says he, 'Look at your seven children, your six-foot sons and your handsome daughters, and think of the little baby lying out in the burying ground. How can you talk about sending the mother of your children to the lunatic asylum, and all because she's undone a little of your work in the last few weeks, when you've been undoing hers all your married life?' Says he, 'You're a hard man, Miles; your nature's like one of the barren, rocky spots you'll come across in one of your pastures — spots where not even a blade of grass can grow.' Says he, 'You can't change your nature any more than the Ethiopian can change his color or the leopard his spots, but from this time on you've got to try to treat Hannah with a little consideration.' And I believe Miles did try. I ricollect seein' him help Hannah put on her shawl one Sunday after church, and pull it around her shoulders mighty awkward, jest as a person would, when he's doin' a thing he never did before. I don't reckon Hannah keered much about it. A man oughtn't to have to try to be kind to his wife, and when a woman comes to the end of a

AN EYE FOR AN EYE

hard life like Hannah's, a little kindness don't amount to much. It's mighty hard to make a thing end right, honey, unless it begins right.

"Hannah got well, though, and the first time she come to church she looked ten years younger; but she never was as strong as she was before she broke down, and I always thought she died before her time. It looked like a curious way to treat a sick person, to put her out in a field and not give her a drop o' medicine, but that was what Hannah wanted, and it made her well. You know the Bible says, 'Hope deferred maketh the heart sick.' And I reckon the cure for that kind o' sickness is havin' the thing you've been hopin' for.

"Hannah said at first she jest laid still with her eyes shut, and felt the wind blowin' over her face, and then she got to droppin' off to sleep every little while, and after she'd begun to feel rested, she'd lay there and look up at the sky and watch the clouds floatin' past, and she said she never knew before how pretty the sky was. She'd been livin' under it all her life and never had time to look up at it.

"Did you ever think, child," said Aunt Jane, breaking off in her story, "that nearly all the work we've got to do keeps us lookin' down? And once in awhile it's a good thing to stop work and look up at the sky. Parson Page used to say that every sunrise and moonrise and sunset was a message from heaven sayin' 'Look up! Look up! for earth is not your home.' Hannah said lookin' up at the sky was like lookin' into deep water, and sometimes she'd feel as if her soul had left her body and she didn't know whether she was still on this earth or whether she'd died and gone to heaven; and she believed if folks would lay off from work once a year and rest under the trees the way she did, they'd live to be as old as Methuselah."

Had I not heard it once before, this homely tale of woman's work and woman's weariness, that life repeats with endless variations? Told in simple rhyme it lay between the yellowed pages of an old scrap-book and hovered half-forgotten in a dusty corner of my brain.

"Aunt Jane," I said, "there was once a woman who felt just as Hannah Crawford did, and she put her feelings into words and called them 'A Woman's Longing:'

"'All hopes, all wishes, all desires have left me,
  My heart is empty as a last year's nest,

AN EYE FOR AN EYE

O, great Earth — Mother! take me to thy bosom
    And give a tired child rest.

" 'Nay, not a grave! Leave thy green turf unbroken!
    Not death I ask, — but strength to bear my life,
This endless round of strange, conflicting duties,
    These stale conventions and this aimless strife.

" ' I have no part nor lot in such existence,
    And I am like a stream cut from its source;
Let me go hence and quench the spirit's thirsting
    At those deep springs of force

" 'That well unseen neath all life's myriad phases,
    Rousing to action, lulling to repose —
A child's first cry, a warrior's call to battle,
    A planet's march, the fading of a rose.

" ' Give me a bed among earth's flowers and grasses,
    Some shadowy place from men and things apart,
Where I can hear and feel the steady beating
    Of Nature's tireless heart,

" ' Stilling the tumult of my brain, o'er-crowded
    With fears and fancies that have banished sleep,
And **losing** pain and weariness forever
    In heaven's unfathomed deep,

" ' Till I lay hold upon my dear lost birth-right,
    My oneness with all things that were and are,

THE LAND OF LONG AGO

Can feel the sea's pulse mine, my breath the wind's breath,
And trace my kinship to the evening star.

" 'Then send me back to life's imperious calling,
The love that crushes and the cares that irk,
To strive, to fail, to strive again and conquer,
Till the night cometh when no man can work.' "

Aunt Jane had dropped her knitting; her eyes glowed, and she leaned forward entranced, for the simple verses held the unfailing spells that rhythm and rhyme have cast over the soul ever since the Muses touched their golden harps on Parnassus, pouring "the dew of soft persuasion on the lips of man" and "dispelling sorrow and grief from the breast of every mortal."

"Why, child," she exclaimed, drawing a breath of deep delight, "that's as pretty as any hymn. But it looks like anybody that can say things that pretty oughtn't to have the troubles that common folks has."

Ah, if the power to put a sorrowful thought into beautiful words brought with it exemption from sorrow, who would not covet the gift?

"But," continued Aunt Jane, "everybody has to have some trials. I ricollect Parson Page preachin' a sermon about that very thing. He said folks in trouble

AN EYE FOR AN EYE

always thought their troubles was more than anybody's; and they'd look around and see somebody that appeared to be happy and they'd envy that person, when maybe that person was envyin' them, for it's jest as the Bible says, ' There hath no trouble taken you but is common to all men.' "

And while Aunt Jane spoke I saw this life of ours as a sacramental feast. The table is long, and here sits a king and there a beggar. The cups are many, and mine may be of clay and yours of gold, but the wine, the bitter-sweet wine, is the same for all. One rapture throbs in the heart of the Romany youth who plights his troth under the forest tree, and the heart of the prince royal who kneels at the cathedral altar. The tramp-wife burying her baby by the roadside might clasp hands with the queen-mother who weeps at the door of the royal mausoleum, for on the heights of joy or in the depths of pain all men are brothers, all women sisters.

"And now, honey," said Aunt Jane, "I've wasted enough o' this pretty mornin' talkin' about old times. Spring time's workin' time and I must be up and doin'."

But I caught her hand and held her fast.

THE LAND OF LONG AGO

"Just one thing more, Aunt Jane," I pleaded. "Tell me what you meant by saying that being the man he was Dr. Pendleton couldn't marry?"

Aunt Jane hesitated a moment looking towards a certain flower-bed where tulips and hyacinths stood half-smothered in a drift of dead leaves. The morning hours were passing and the garden needed the work of her hands, but my clasp was firm and the call of the past was still sounding in her heart.

"I meant jest what I said, honey," she answered, settling herself again on the old garden seat. "There's such a thing as a man lovin' a woman too well to marry her, and that's the way it was with the doctor. You might think, maybe, Dr. Pendleton come of plain folks, bein' jest a country doctor. But, no; his people was among the best and the richest in the county, and he'd had all the chances that rich people can give their children. He'd been to college and he'd travelled around and seen the world, and no young man could 'a' had a prettier prospect before him than Arthur Pendleton, — that was the doctor's name, — when he come home from his studyin' and his travellin' and started out to practisin' medicine with his father. Young and handsome and rich, and then there

AN EYE FOR AN EYE

was Miss Dorothy Schuyler, and he was in love with her and she was in love with him. Father used to say when a man had all that, there wasn't standin' room for a wish.

"Miss Dorothy was one o' the Virginia Schuylers, and the first time she come to visit her Kentucky cousins, she met the young doctor, and they fell in love with each other jest like Hamilton Schuyler and Miss Amaryllis, and before she went back to her home it was all settled that they'd be married the next spring. The young doctor, he made a journey to Virginia to git her father's and mother's consent; for in that day and time, child, a young man couldn't jest pick up a gyirl and walk off with her. He had to say 'By your leave' and do a little courtin' with the old folks before he could claim the gyirl.

"Well, it all looked like plain sailin' for the young doctor. His father begun givin' up his practice — took off his own shoes, you might say, and let his son step into 'em — and the weddin' day was comin', when all at once the banks got to failin' all over the country, and the Pendletons lost pretty near everything they had except their land. Then, to make a bad matter worse, the old doctor's name was on a note, and that fell due about the time the banks failed, and he had to sell the family place and a good deal o' the land.

"They said when he got through settlin' up his affairs he says, 'Well, I've lost my money and my lands and my home, but I've saved my good name.'

"I reckon it must 'a' taken the young doctor a good while to come to an understandin' of what he'd lost. By the time you're old, losin' comes natural to you, but it's hard for young folks to take in a big loss. But as soon as Arthur Pendleton understood that all his father had was a good name, and all he had was his father's practice, he wrote to Miss Dorothy and set her free from her promise to marry him.

"The old doctor begged him not to do it. Says he, 'Son, you've lost pretty near everything, and now you're throwing away the best of what's left.' Says he, 'Don't strip your life bare of every chance for happiness. Hold on to love, even if you have lost your money.'

"But the young doctor says, says he, 'When a man's money's gone it's no time for him to be thinkin' about love.' Says he, 'Unless a man loves a woman well enough to give her up when he's too poor to take care of her, his love's not worth much. In her father's house,' says he, ' she's lived like the lilies of the field, and the man that loves her mustn't be the one to bring her down to poverty and hard work.' So he wrote to her and told her to forget him as soon as she could, and love some other man who could give her what a woman ought to have, and she told him that if she ever loved anybody else, she'd send back the ring he'd given her. But, honey, that ring stayed on Miss Dorothy's finger till her dyin' day, and I reckon it was buried with her. Folks said they never wrote to each other any more, but every year or so Miss Dorothy'd come back to visit the Schuylers and the doctor he'd go to see her, and they used to say that he'd look at her finger before he'd look at her face, and when he'd see his ring there he'd be too happy to say a word. He'd take both her hands in his, and his eyes'd fill up with tears and he'd look down at her face, and she'd look up at him and laugh and ask him if he didn't want his ring back to give to some other gyirl.

"Well, things went on this way one year after another, the doctor workin' and Miss Dorothy comin' and goin' and both of 'em hopin', I reckon, and lookin' forward to marryin' some day; for she was young and so was he, and when folks are young they always feel certain of havin' their own way with life, and it's easy for 'em to wait and hope for the things that's out o' reach. But nothin' seemed to go right with the doctor. If he saved up a little money and put it in the bank, or bought a piece o' property, bad luck was sure to come along and pull down everything he'd built up. His father's health broke down, and of course he had to ease the old man's way to the grave; his youngest brother had to be educated, and first one thing and then another kept comin' up and puttin' Miss Dorothy further off.

"But the older they got, the more they loved each other; and Miss Dorothy, she'd come and go every summer, till finally one summer she didn't come; and the next summer the doctor went to Virginia to see her, and come back lookin' like an old, old man; and not long afterwards he come into church one Sunday with a band o' black crape around his hat, and then we knew Miss Dorothy was dead."

"But wasn't Miss Dorothy willing to marry the doctor in spite of his poverty?" I asked.

"I reckon she must 'a' been," responded Aunt Jane. "When a woman waits all her life for a man, like Miss

AN EYE FOR AN EYE

Dorothy did for the doctor, it stands to reason she's willin' to marry him any time."

"Oh! Then why in the world didn't she tell him so?" I exclaimed.

The bodies of my lovers were dust and their souls with the saints these many years, but Aunt Jane had called from the dead "each frustrate ghost"; the pathos of her tale thrilled me sharply and I could not stay my cry of regret over "The counter these lovers staked" — and lost.

Aunt Jane turned toward me and looked over her glasses with frank astonishment in her clear old eyes. More than once had I shocked her with sentiments discordant with her own ideals of life and conduct, but never so severely as now. She delayed her reply as if to give me a gracious opportunity to recall my unseemly words. Then —

"Child," she said, in a low voice, "you know such a thing wouldn't be fittin' for a young gyirl to do. Why that'd be pretty near as bad as Miss Dorothy askin' the doctor to marry her. No matter how much a woman loves a man, she's got to sit still and wait till he asks her to marry him, and if he never asks her, why, all she can do is to marry somebody else or stay an old maid. With the raisin' you've had, I oughtn't to have to tell you that."

"Oh! Of course!" I hastily assented. "A woman can't ask a man to marry her. But isn't it sad to see people losing their happiness in this way?"

"Now, that's the curious part of it, child," said Aunt Jane. "It's mighty mournful while I'm tellin' it, but if you'd known the doctor and Miss Dorothy, you never would 'a' thought they were losin' anything. At first, you must ricollect, they had hopes to keep their spirits up, and as long as you've got hope, child, you've got everything. Of course there must 'a' come a time when they stopped hopin', and I reckon that was when their hair begun to turn gray and their eyesight failed. It's a time that comes to all of us, honey, and when it does come, we generally find that we've got grace to give up the things we've been wantin' so long; and that's the way it was with Miss Dorothy and the doctor. To see them two, after they'd passed their youth, walkin' together and ridin' together and comin' into church and settin' side by side in the same pew, singin' out o' the same hymn book, — why it was the prettiest sight in the world. Mighty few old married couples ever looked as happy as Miss Dorothy

AN EYE FOR AN EYE

and the doctor, old maid and old bachelor as they were.

"Plenty of folks, though, thought jest as you do, and Mother was one of 'em. She never had any patience with the way Dr. Pendleton and Miss Dorothy behaved about marryin'. Says she, 'You put an old married woman and an old maid together, and you can't tell which is which. A woman's got to lose her good looks and her health whether she marries or not, and while she's about it, she might as well lose 'em for her husband and her children instead o' stayin' single and dryin' up all for nothin'.' They said Judge Elrod undertook to reason with the doctor once about the folly of two people stayin' single when they loved each other. He p'inted out to him that Miss Dorothy was gittin' on in years, and that a woman ought to be willin' to put up with a few hardships if she loved a man. And the doctor, he listened, and shook his head and says he, 'Yes, she's fading, fading, but — God be thanked! — it's no fault of mine. The hand of time has touched her; her pretty curls are turning gray and the pretty color's leaving her cheek; but her hands are as soft and white as they were when I put my ring on her finger. She's never known a hardship or carried a burden. She'll go to her grave like a rose that's touched by the frost, and I can bear to be parted from her that way. But if I'd put a hardship or a burden on her and she'd died under it, I'd never be able to look my own soul in the face.'

"That's the way he looked at it, and nothin' could ever make him change his mind. I reckon the doctor's way o' lovin' was somethin' like Hamilton Schuyler's."

With these words Aunt Jane closed the treasure-chest of memory and walked briskly away to look after the welfare of the tulips and hyacinths.

A little story of a great love! And as I pondered it, the country doctor became a knight of a finer chivalry than that which once stirred the blood under a coat of mail, or guided a lance-thrust to an enemy's heart. In every man's soul there is a field of valor, lonely, perhaps unknown; and he is the true knight who enters the lists against himself and strikes down every impulse of man's nature that would harm the woman he loves. And how rich the guerdon of such a victory, and the recompense of the beloved one for whose sake he strives and conquers!

The pitying world looks on and measures the unwed

AN EYE FOR AN EYE

lovers' loss, but who can measure their gain? Theirs is the bliss which Psyche had before she lit the fatal lamp. They hold forever in their hearts "the consecration and the poet's dream"; and, undimmed by disillusionment, the mirage of youthful love hovers over each solitary path, lighting the twilight of age, the night of death and melting at last into the dawn of heaven's unending day.

VII

THE REFORMATION
OF SAM AMOS

VII

THE REFORMATION OF SAM AMOS

ALL day the land had lain dreamily under an enchantment soon to be broken by the rude counter-spells of the coming winter.

A frost so light that it was hardly more than a cold dew had rested that morning on the early chrysanthemums and late roses; but the wind that shook the leaves from the crimson maples was a south wind; the midday sun held the tropic warmth of August, and over the brightening hills lay a tender, purple haze. Summer was dead, but its gentle ghost had come back to the earth, and it was Indian summer, the season that has no name or place in any calendar but the poet's. The sun had set, and the mist that veiled the horizon had caught its last rays, holding the light lingeringly, fondly, in its folds and spreading it far to the north and south in a soft splendor of color that no other season can show. Not pink, not crimson, but such a color as an artist might make if he crushed together on his palette the rose of summer and the leaf of autumn. The chill of the coming night was in the air, but still we lingered at the gate, Aunt Jane and I, with our faces toward the west.

"I wonder how many folks are watchin' this sunset," she remarked at last. "Old Job Matthews, after he got converted at the big revival back yonder in the thirties, used to look for the second comin' of the Lord, and every sunset and sunrise he'd stand and look at the sky and say, 'Maybe the King of Glory is at hand.' Once the old man declared he saw a chariot in the clouds, and it does look like, child, that somethin' ought to happen after a sight like this, or

THE REFORMATION OF AMOS

else it ain't worth while to git it up jest for a few people like you and me to look at."

As she spoke there was a quick, sharp clang of hoofs on the macadamized road, and a horse and rider passed in the twilight. The clean, even gait of the horse and the outlines of its head showed it to be of noble blood; and as it trotted past with an air of proud alertness, we could see that the dumb animal realized the double share of responsibility laid upon it. For the hand that held the bridle was limp and nerveless, the rider's head was sunk on his breast, and the brain of the man that should have guided the brain of the horse was locked in a poison-stupor.

Long and wistfully Aunt Jane gazed after the horse and its rider, and the gathering darkness could not hide the divine sorrow and pity that looked out from her aged eyes. Sighing heavily she turned from the gate, and we went back to the shadowy room where the "unlit lamp" and the unkindled fire lay ready for the evening hours.

The fireplace was filled with brush cleared that day from the flower-beds, dry stems that had borne the verdure and bloom of a spring and now lay on their funeral pyre, ready to be translated, as by a chariot

THE LAND OF LONG AGO

of fire, into the elemental air and earth from whence they had sprung.

Aunt Jane struck a match under the old mantel and, stooping, touched the dead mass with the finger of flame.

Ah! the first fires of autumn! There is more than light and more than heat in their radiance. But as I watched the flames leap with exultant roar into the gloom of the old chimney, my heart was with the lonely man homeward bound, his sorrowful, helpless figure a silhouette against the sunset sky, and Aunt Jane, too, looked with absent eyes at the fire she had just kindled.

"Yes, child," she said, answering my thought, "it's a sad, sad sight; I've watched it for a lifetime and I'm clean tired of it, — seein' 'em go out in the mornin' straight and strong and handsome as a Kentucky man ought to be, and comin' home at night with hardly strength enough to handle their reins, and less sense than the horse that's carryin' 'em. I trust that man'll reach home safe, for somewhere up the road there's a woman waitin' for him. She's cooked a hot supper for him and the biscuits are in the pan, and she's put the coffee on the back o' the stove to keep it from

THE REFORMATION OF AMOS

boilin' too long, and the meat's in the dish in front o' the stove, and she's lookin' out o' the window and goin' to the gate every few minutes, strainin' her eyes and her ears lookin' down the road and listenin' for the sound of a horse's feet. And maybe there's a baby asleep in the cradle, and another child waitin' for Father; and when he comes, the child'll run from him, and his wife'll cry her eyes out, and nobody in that house'll feel like eatin' any supper to-night. Well, may the Lord give that woman grace to be as patient with her husband as Milly Amos was with Sam, and maybe she'll reap the same reward."

"Was Sam Amos a drunkard?" I asked in surprise.

"Well, no," said Aunt Jane, judicially, "Sam wasn't, to say, a drunkard. A drunkard, according to my notion, is a man that's born with whiskey in his veins. He's elected and predestined to drink, you might say, and he ain't to be blamed when he does drink. Sam wasn't that sort of a man; but once in his life it looked mightily like he was goin' to be a drunkard. Sam come of a sober family, and there wasn't any manner of reason for him to take to drink, but Dr. Pendleton used to say there was a wild streak in nearly every person, and sooner or later it was bound to break out

THE LAND OF LONG AGO

in one way or another. It was the wild streak in Brother Wilson, I reckon, that sent him into the army before he went to preachin', and the same wild streak put it into Sam's mind to drink whiskey, when his father and grandfather never touched it. How it started I don't know, but I reckon the coffee house must 'a' been the beginnin' of it. I can ricollect well the time when that was opened in town. They had a sort of a debatin' society in that day, — Lyceum, they called it, but Sam Amos called it the Jawin' Club. Dr. Brigham and Judge Grace and Judge Elrod and Colonel Walker and all the big men o' the town belonged to it, and they used to meet in the doctor's office and argue about everything that was done in the town or the State. One question they had up was whether the Whigs or the Democrats had the best party, and they argued till pretty near one o'clock in the mornin', and the meetin' come mighty near breakin' up in a fight. Well, when the coffee-house got its license they had a debate about that, and Dr. Brigham, he was in favor of the license, he got up to make a speech, and, says he, 'What would this State be without whiskey?' And Judge Grace, he was against it, — he jumped up and shook his fist at the doctor and

THE REFORMATION OF AMOS

says he, 'A heap more peaceable place than it is with it.' And that made the doctor mad, but he went on like he hadn't heard it. Says he, 'You jest shut your eyes and say the word "Kentucky," and what'll you see? Why, you'll see a glass o' toddy or a mint julep, and a pretty woman smilin' over 'em,' — and Judge Grace he hollers out, 'No, you won't! No, you won't! You may see the toddy and the julep and the woman, but the woman won't be smilin'; she'll be cryin' her eyes out over the stuff that makes a brute of her husband and her son.' This made the doctor madder still, but he kept right on, and says he, 'Think of the poetry that's been written about wine and whiskey —

> "' " Fill up, fill up
> The brimmin' cup " —

and all the rest o' the songs about drinkin'! And no wonder,' says he, 'for where'll you find a prettier sight than a clear glass tumbler with a sprig o' mint and a silver spoon in it and two or three lumps o' sugar dissolvin' in the julep?' And the Judge says, 'All right! All right! Keep your toddy and your julep in a glass tumbler and look at 'em and write poetry about 'em, and I won't say a word against 'em. But,' says he, 'when they get inside of a man, where's your poetry then?' Says he, 'It'll take some mighty plain prose to fit that situation,' says he.

"Well, they had it up and down and back and forth, and finally their friends had to hold 'em to keep 'em from comin' to blows. But as I was sayin', that coffee house was the beginnin' of Sam Amos's troubles and Milly's. The coffee house was a sociable sort of a place, and Sam was a sociable sort of a man, and it was natural for him to go there and see his friends and talk with 'em, and the first thing we knew he was drinkin' with 'em; not much, but enough to unsettle his brain and make him talk wild and act foolish. And he went on followin' the same old beaten track that men 'a' been walkin' since the days of Noah. And at last he got to neglectin' his farm, and he'd go to town every week and come home in such a condition that it wasn't safe for Milly and the children to be in the same house with him. Folks used to say that the first drink made Sam a fool, and the second drink made him a devil, and the third drink put the fool and the devil to sleep.

"Sam was as smart a man as you'd find anywhere, and many a time I used to feel for Milly when he'd mortify her before company by sayin' foolish things he never would 'a' said if he'd been in his right senses. I ricollect once she had a parlor full o' company and she was showin' an ambrotype of her brother David, and somebody passed it to Sam and he took it and looked at it right hard, and says he, ' Shuh! that don't look half as much like Dave as he looks like himself.' And another time, one county court day, me and Abram happened to be standin' on the corner in front o' the old drug store, and Sam come a staggerin' up and laid his hand on Abram's shoulder and looked him straight in the eye like he had somethin' mighty important to say, and says he, ' Uncle Abram, I want to tell you right here and now, and don't you ever forgit it; if there's anything I do despise it's one thing more'n another.' I don't believe Abram ever got through laughin' at that. And if Sam had only stopped at the first glass that made a fool of him, his drinkin' would 'a' been a small matter. But the man that can stop at one glass don't live in Kentucky, child, and so Sam went from the first glass to the second and from the second to the third and from that to the gutter. And many a time the neighbors had to pick Sam up and bring him home, for betwixt the shame of seein' him in that condition

THE LAND OF LONG AGO

and the danger of bein' with him, Milly had to stop goin' to town.

"I ricollect one county court day me and Abram happened to be passin' along in front o' the old Methodist Church, and Sam come walkin' out o' Jockey Alley leadin' his big bay mare — Jockey Alley, child, is the alley that runs from State Street clean back to the street leadin' over to the old footbridge, and everybody that had a horse or a mule or a colt to swap, why, they'd go to that alley and do their swappin' every county court day.

"Well, as I was sayin', Sam come along leadin' his bay mare. That mare was the pride of Sam's heart. He used to say there was more good blood in that bay mare of his than in any six families in the state o' Kentucky. Sam was a mighty fine judge o' horse flesh, and he got his love for horses from his father and his grandfather, old Harrison Amos. The old man was one o' the biggest horse raisers in the state, and he made his thousands out of it, too. But folks that went to his farm used to say it was like huntin' a hen's nest to find the house where the family lived, the house was so little and there was so many big fine barns and stables. Somebody asked him once why he didn't build a better house for his children to live in, and the old man says, 'I believe in puttin' my money where I am certain of gettin' good returns.' Says he, 'There's no manner of certainty in children. You can put good blood into a boy and do your best to bring him up in the way he should go, and after all you've spent on him he'll lose every race he goes into, and you'll find you've got a scrub on your hands. But,' says he, 'you breed a horse right, and train him in his gaits whilst he's young, and there ain't one chance in a thousand of your losin' money on that horse. Of course,' says he, 'I think more of my boys than I do of my horses, but when it comes to investin' money, a man must be governed by his judgment and his common sense, not by his feelin's.'

"They said the old man went down to New Orleans one winter on some business and left his son Joe in charge o' the stock farm, and when he got back he went out to the stables, the first thing, to look at his horses, and when he got through, there was four of his thoroughbreds missin'. And, says he, 'Joe, where's May Queen?' and Joe says, 'Why, Father, she's dead; died right after you left.' And the old man said, 'Well, where's Dixie Gyirl,' and Joe says, 'Why,

Father, I'm mighty sorry to have to tell you, but Dixie Gyirl, she's dead, — died pretty near the same time May Queen died.' And the old man says, 'Well, where's Annie Laurie and Nelly Gray?' And Joe says, 'Father, I'm mighty sorry, but they died just like Dixie Gyirl and May Queen.' And the old man looked at Joe for a minute, and says he, right slow and earnest, 'Well, Joe, why didn't you die, too?'

"So that's where Sam got his love o' fine horses, child, and, as I was sayin', Sam come walkin' up leadin' his bay mare by the bridle. Me and Abram on our way to the drug store and Tige, our yeller house-dog, follerin' close behind us, and Sam called to us to stop, and says he, 'Can't we make a trade to-day? I'll swap you my mare for your dog.' And Abram says, 'Done,' and he took hold o' the mare's bridle, and he pulled a piece o' stout twine out of his pocket and tied it to Tige's collar and put the end o' the string in Sam's hand. I says to him, 'Why, Abram, you wouldn't take advantage of a poor drunken man, and a neighbor at that?' And Abram says, 'Make yourself easy, Jane, I'm only goin' to give Sam a lesson that may shame him out of his drinkin' habits for awhile, at least.' And then he led the mare to the stable and told

THE REFORMATION OF AMOS

the man to feed her and water her, and he'd call for her late that evenin'.

"Well, when goin'-home time come round, we set out to look for Sam, and after lookin' all around the Square and up and down Main Street, we found him lyin' helpless in the back o' the grocery store. Abram got two men to help him, and they managed to lift him up and put him in the wagon. Then we drove around to the livery stable and got the bay mare and fastened her to the back o' the wagon and started home. When we got to our gate, Abram put me and the children out and turned Sam's mare into the horse lot, and then he drove over to Sam's farm as quick as he could, for he knew Milly was waitin' and grievin'. And sure enough there she was, standin' under the big sycamore in front o' the gate, lookin' and listenin' for Sam. She told me afterwards she'd stayed out that way many a night till her clothes'd be wet with the dew, and for the rest of her life she hated the sound of crickets and katydids, because they reminded her of that year when Sam give her so much trouble.

"Well, Abram drove up to the gate, and Milly was too skeered to speak. She was always worryin' about Sam fallin' off his horse and breakin' his neck, and when she saw Abram and nobody with him, she thought he was comin' on ahead to break the news to her, and Sam's dead body would be the next thing to come. Abram didn't know this, or he'd a told her right at once that Sam was in the wagon. He said when he stopped, Milly was leanin' forward, her hands together, and hardly enough breath to speak, and she whispered, 'Where's Sam?' And Abram says, 'Right here in the wagon.' And Milly says, 'Thank God! I was afraid he was dead.' Now that shows what kind of a heart Milly had. When a man's brought home dead drunk, child, it ain't every woman that'll thank God he's alive.

"Well, they had some trouble rousin' Sam, but at last they got him to the house and took off his coat and shoes and laid him on the bed, and when Abram started to go Milly says, 'But where's Sam's mare?' And Abram says, 'When Sam comes to himself to-morrow, you send him over to my house and I'll put him on the track of his mare.' So the next mornin' about eleven o'clock here was Sam lookin' about as reckless and miserable as a man ever gits to look, and says he, 'I've come for my mare, Uncle Abram; I see the stable door's open, so you needn't bother yourself;

THE REFORMATION OF AMOS

I'll go down there and saddle her and ride her home. I'm much obliged to you,' says he, 'for takin' care of her.'

"And Abram says, 'Sam, you may not know it, but that mare belongs to me.' And Sam laughed and says he, 'I reckon I do owe you somethin' for bringin' me home last night, but you surely won't take my horse for that.' And Abram says, 'But, Sam, you swapped that mare to me yesterday,' and Sam says, 'Swapped her? What did I swap her for?' And jest then old Tige come around the corner o' the house waggin' his tail, and Abram p'inted to him and says he, 'You swapped your mare for that dog, Sam.'

"Well, for a minute Sam couldn't say a word he was so thunderstruck, and says he, 'Do you mean to say, Uncle Abram, that I was such a fool yesterday as to swap my bay mare, the finest piece o' horse flesh in the State, for that old yeller dog, and me the best judge of horses in Warren County?' 'Yes,' says Abram, 'you did that very thing, Sam, and the swap was your own proposin'.'

"Well, Sam set down on the door step and folded his arms over his knees and dropped his head on his arm, and he cursed himself and he cursed the whiskey

THE LAND OF LONG AGO

and he cursed the coffee house and finally, says he, 'I swear, I'll never touch another drop o' the cursed stuff, and all the devils in hell can't make me break my oath.'

"And Abram says, 'Well, Sam, I wanted to hear you make that promise, and that's why I kept your mare. Now, go to the stable and you'll find your mare all safe and sound and the saddle and bridle on the right hand side o' the door. And may God give you grace,' says he, 'to keep you from ever makin' such a fool of yourself again.'

"But, honey, it wasn't a month before Sam had to be hauled home again in a wagon. And finally it got to the pass that he come home drunk, late one Monday night, and struck Milly and kicked the children out o' the house, and the next thing we heard was that Milly's father had come to take her home. Milly told me about it long after the trouble was over. She **said** she'd been hopin' that the bruise on her cheek would be well before her father saw her, and she'd been puttin' cold water and hot water and everything else she could think of on it to draw the blood out, but somebody told the old man how bad things had been goin' with Milly, and it wasn't two hours till he

THE REFORMATION OF AMOS

was there with a two horse wagon to move Milly back home. Milly said Sam was sittin' by the table with his head down on his arms and she was washin' up the dinner dishes, and her face bound up in one o' Sam's handkerchiefs. The old man come in, his hands and his lips tremblin', and says he, 'Daughter, put your things together as quick as you can, I've come to take you back home.' Says he, 'I'm no advocate of married folks separatin', but,' says he, 'when Sam took you from your father's house he promised to be good and kind to you, but he's broke his promise, and you've got no call to stay with him any longer.' And Milly said before she could answer him, Sam raised up his head from the table and says he, 'That's right! That's right! I'm not fit to be trusted with a wife and children. Take Milly and the boys with you and leave me to go to the dogs where I belong.' And Milly's father says, 'Well, Samuel, I'm glad you think as I do, for that makes it easier for all of us.' And then he turns to Milly and says he, 'Hurry up, daughter, and get yourself ready to go back home with me. No child of mine shall live with a drunken brute that lays violent hands on his wife and children.'

"I reckon the old man thought he was sayin' exactly the right thing and that Milly would thank him for takin' her part. But Milly said when her father called Sam 'a drunken brute' she was so mad she lifted her hand to strike him, and she run to Sam and put her arms around him, and says she, 'Father, you're the only person in this world that'd dare to say such a thing to me about Sam.' Says she, 'You can take the children if you want to, for I am afraid that Sam'll do them some harm, when he ain't himself, but as for me, my place,' says she, 'is right here with Sam. Drinkin' whiskey is bad enough,' says she, 'but it ain't the worst thing a man can do, and it's not what a man does when he's drunk that makes a woman hate him and leave him, it's what he does when he's sober. And you know,' says she, 'that when Sam's himself there ain't a kinder, better husband anywhere, and no matter what he does when he's drunk, I'll stay with him while life lasts.'

"Milly said Sam give a gasp and looked up at her as if he couldn't believe his ears, and then he burst out cryin' and fell on his knees and threw his arms around her and held on to her like a drownin' man tryin' to save himself. And says he, 'O Milly! Milly! I didn't know you cared that much for me! I've asked

THE REFORMATION OF AMOS

God to help me,' says he, ' and He didn't seem to care, but if you care enough to stay with me, Milly, I'll have to quit! I'll have to quit! ' says he.

"Milly said if it had been little Sam holdin' on to her and beggin' her to stay she couldn't 'a' felt sorrier for him, and she patted him on the head and says she, ' Don't you worry, Sam; Father may take the children if he wants to, but he'll never take me. Of course, you're goin' to quit drinkin',' says she, ' but whether you quit or not I'll stand by you, for that's what a wife's for.'

"Milly said Sam cried still harder, and her father, he wiped his eyes and says he, ' Well, daughter, maybe you're right. Meddlin' with married folks' affairs is a poor business, anyhow, and I'm more than willin' to give Samuel another chance.'

"So the old man got in his wagon and drove off, and Milly said all that day Sam stayed around the house and follered her about like a dog follerin' its master, and every now and then he'd say, ' I've got to quit, Milly, and I will quit now.' Milly said she'd heard him promise that so often and break his promise that she didn't have a bit of faith that he'd keep it now, but of course she didn't let him know it. She'd say,

'Why, of course you will, Sam, I've always believed you'd quit sometime.' And Sam says, 'Keep on believin' in me, Milly, and your faith'll save me.'

"Well, the very next Monday was county court day, and all day Sunday Milly told me she was prayin' that Sam would be kept from goin' to town. But right after supper Sam says, 'I'm goin' to town to-morrow, Milly. Make your arrangements for goin' with me — you and the children — and we'll get an early start.'

"Milly said she couldn't sleep much that night, and she prayed that it might pour down rain, or somethin' would happen to keep Sam at home. But the sun come up clear, and there was nothin' to do but dress and go to town with Sam. She said Sam took particular pains with himself, put on his Sunday clothes, and shaved and combed and brushed his hair till he looked more like his old self than he'd looked since he took to drinkin'. She said the road to town never had seemed so short and she kept hopin' somethin' would happen to send Sam back home, but nothin' happened, and when they struck the Square, Sam went right down Main Street right in the direction of the coffee house. Milly said her heart give a jump and she shook all over like she was havin' a chill, but

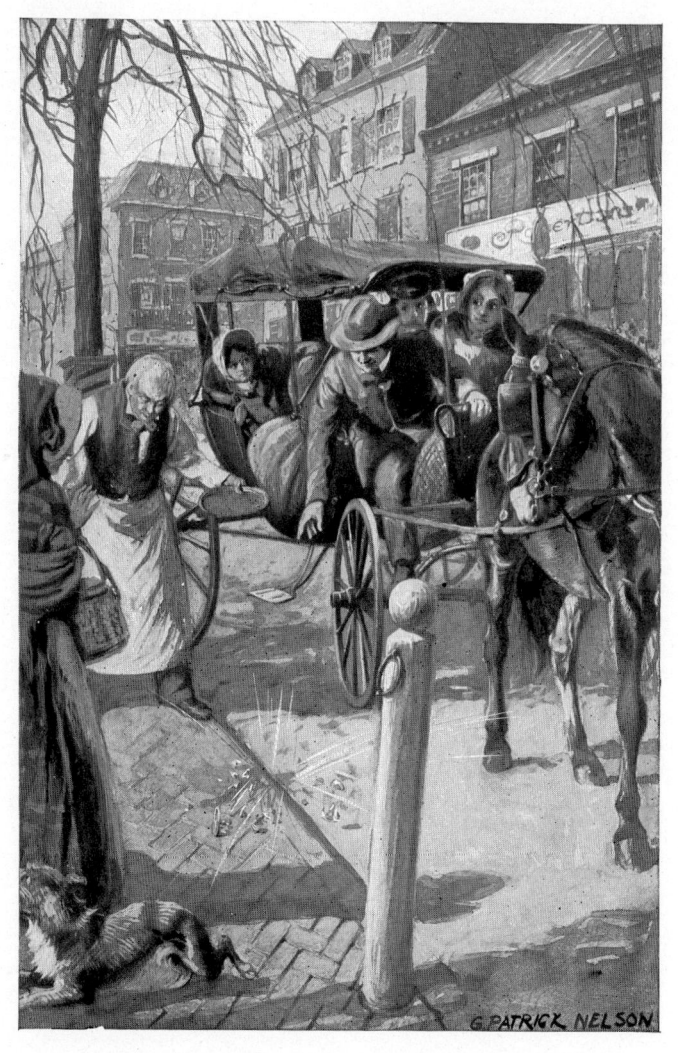

"'THE GLASS BROKE INTO A HUNDRED PIECES.'"
Page 229.

THE REFORMATION OF AMOS

she didn't say a word, because she knew if Sam had made up his mind to drink that day, she couldn't stop him. And sure enough he went on and stopped right in front of the coffee house. The barkeeper was standin' in the door, and Sam called out to him and says, 'Fix me up a glass o' that old Bourbon the way I like it and bring it out here to me.' And the barkeeper went in and fixed it up and come out with it, smilin' as a basket o' chips, and handed it to Sam.

"Sam had his purse out and says he, 'How much is the glass worth?' And the barkeeper says, 'About five cents, I reckon.' And Sam handed over the money for the drink and the glass, and then he held the glass up and looked at it, and he put his face down and smelled it, and then he put it to his lips like he intended to drink it, and then he turned around to Milly and says, 'Look here, Milly!' and he dashed it down in the gutter, and the glass broke into a hundred pieces, and the whiskey spattered on the horse's hoofs and the barkeeper's shoes. Milly said Sam was as white as a ghost and shakin' as hard as she was, and he nodded to the barkeeper and says he, 'That's my last drink.' And then he turned around and drove up the street towards the Square.

THE LAND OF LONG AGO

"Milly said she was so thankful he hadn't touched the whiskey that she begun cryin' for joy, but still she didn't know whether that was his last drink or not, he'd broken so many promises to her before. And Sam seemed to know what was in her mind, for he says to her, 'Milly, do you believe me or not?' And Milly said all at once she thought o' that text o' scripture that says, 'For by grace are ye saved through faith.' And she thought o' Sam the day her Father come to take her home and how he kept sayin', 'Keep on believin' in me, Milly, and your faith'll save me.' And she laid her hand on Sam's knee and says she, 'Yes, Sam, I do believe you.' And the minute she spoke the word, she said it looked like a stone rolled away from her heart, and she felt in her soul that she'd come to the end of her trouble, and the world appeared to be made over and made new. When they got to the Square Sam handed her a roll o' bills and says he, 'Now go and buy yourself and the children some Christmas gifts, while I lay in the groceries we need, and then we'll meet at the drug store and go home whenever you're ready to go.'

"Milly said she took the money and bought things for the children, but when she begun to look in the

THE REFORMATION OF AMOS

windows and the show cases for somethin' for herself, she couldn't see a thing that would make her any happier than she was, so she put the rest o' the money in the waist of her dress and when Sam met her in front o' the drug store she handed it to him and says she, 'I've bought the children some things, but there's no use wastin' money on a woman who's got everything on earth she wants.' So she wouldn't let Sam buy her a thing that Christmas, and yet, she said she felt as if she owned the whole earth.

"And, honey, when Sam dashed that glass o' whiskey to the ground and said that was his last drink, he told the truth, and if he'd been the chief of sinners there couldn't 'a' been more rejoicin' over him as the time went by, and everybody in Goshen begun to feel sure that he'd quit for good. Parson Page said somethin' to him one day about the grace of God savin' him. And Sam shook his head and says he, 'No, Parson, I'm certain God's too honest to want credit that don't belong to him, and in the matter of my quittin' drink, it wasn't the grace of God that stopped me, it was the grace of my wife, Milly.' And Doctor Pendleton was standin' by and says he, 'Yes, all Sam needed was a great moral uplift. The grace of God might have given

THE LAND OF LONG AGO

it, but,' says he, ' in a case like his there's no lever like a woman's love.'

"But I never got through wonderin' over the way Milly bore with Sam in the days when he was walkin' the downward path and it looked like nothin' could stop him. Human nature is a curious thing, child. You may think you know a person so well that you can tell exactly what he'll do, if a certain thing happens; but many and many time I've found myself mistaken about folks I'd known all my life, and it was that way with Milly. Milly was high-tempered and quick-spoken, and if anybody had asked me how Milly would act if Sam took to drinkin', I'd 'a' said at once, ' Why, she'd leave him that quick.' But she didn't; she was as patient with him as any mother ever was with her son. She'd put him to bed and wait on him, and when he'd come to himself she'd never say a word about what had happened, and I reckon it was her grace that saved him.

"And, it's another curious thing, child," she continued, " how two people'll live together for years and years and never know how much they love each other. Milly told me that when Sam burst out cryin' and said he didn't know she cared that much for him, it

THE REFORMATION OF AMOS

come over her all at once that she must 'a' been a mighty poor sort o' wife to him, for him not to know she loved him well enough to stay with him through thick and thin. But I reckon it's that way with most married folks. They jog along together, and they have their ups and downs, and may be they think many a time they don't love each other like they did when they first married, but jest let a trouble come up, and they'll find out that all the love they used to have is there yet, and more besides.

"I ricollect Parson Page sayin' once that love and money was alike in one respect, they'd both draw interest, and I reckon many a married couple's richer than they think they are."

To find our treasure of love greater than we had dared to dream — what rarer joy has earth? And when the poor derelict soul clung to his wife and found in her a help sufficient for his needs, his was a rapture not less profound than that of the poet-husband when he opened the sonnets in which a woman's soul had poured itself, counting the ways and measuring the depth and the height of her wifely love.

Aunt Jane pushed her spectacles up on her forehead, folded her hands, and leaned back in her chair, lost

THE LAND OF LONG AGO

in the reverie that generally followed the telling of a story, while I gazed at the tremulous fire light, and felt the cord of human sympathy drawing me closer to the people of her day and time.

As an artist finishes a picture, and then goes lovingly back to strengthen a line or deepen a tint, so every story told by Aunt Jane made more vivid to me her portraits of these men and women who were the friends of her youth. I had known Sam, the jovial, careless, sceptical one; Milly, quick of temper, sharp of tongue, swift to act and swift to repent — just a plain farmer and a plain farmer's wife. But by the light of this tale of triumph I saw them again. Sam, the man who met and vanquished the dragon of thirst, Milly, the woman whose love was strong enough to hold and redeem; and in my thought each rises to heroic stature and stands touched forevermore " with something of an angel light." For it is not battles that drench the earth with the blood of her sons, but these unchronicled victories of the spirit that lift man from the clod to the star and make him even greater than the angels.

VIII
IN WAR TIME

VIII

IN WAR TIME

THE sun that morning had touched the gold of the daffodils with promise of a clear day; but before it was half way to its meridian hour, the air grew chill, the wind veered suddenly to the northeast, the sky darkened angrily, and out of the clouds, like white petals from some celestial orchard, came a flurry of great, soft snow flakes that rested for a moment on the young grass and the golden daffodils and then dissolved into a gentle dew, to be gathered again into the chalice of the air and given back to the earth as an April shower.

There was a strange, bewildering beauty in the scene. The tender, delicate foliage of early spring was on every bough, the long wands of peach trees were pink with bloom, daffodils and hyacinths sprang at our feet, and we looked at leaf and flower through a storm of snow flakes that ceased as suddenly as it had begun, and with a brightening sky and a warmer wind it was April again.

Aunt Jane drew a long breath of delight.

"Well, child," she said, "there's always somethin' new to be seen in this world of ours. Old as I am, I never did see exactly such a sight as this, and maybe it'll be a life time as long as mine before anybody sees it again. Such big, soft lookin' flakes o' snow! It looks like they'd be warm if you touched 'em, and fallin' all over the flowers and young grass. Why, it's the prettiest sight I ever did see." And, with a lingering look at the sky and the earth, Aunt Jane turned away and went back to the work of cleaning out a closet in the front room, a task preliminary to

IN WAR TIME

the spring cleaning that was to come a little later. There was a pile of boxes and bundles on the floor, and she was drawing strange things from the depth of the closet.

"Some o' these days," she remarked, "there'll be a house-cleanin' in this house, and I won't be here. I'll be lyin' out in the old buryin' ground along-side of Abram; and my children and grandchildren, they'll be goin' through the closet and the bureau drawers like I'm doin' to-day, and every time I clean house, thinks I to myself: 'I'll make their work jest as light as I can;' so I git rid of all the rubbish, burn it up or give it away to somebody that can use it. But after all my burnin' and givin', I reckon there'll be a plenty of useless things left behind me. Here's this Shaker bonnet; now what's the use o' savin' such a thing? But every time I look at it I think o' Friend Fanny Lacy and the rest o' the old Shakers, whose like we'll never see again, and somehow I keep holdin' on to it."

She thrust her hand into the bonnet, and holding it off, regarded it with a look of deep affection. The straw was yellow with age, and the lining and strings were faded and time-stained; but looking at it she saw the Shakers in shining garments, going through the streets of the old town, in the days when the spirit of Mother Ann burned in the souls of her followers and the blessing of heaven rested on Shakertown.

Sighing gently, she laid the precious relic aside and took up the song she was singing when I called her to the porch to see the April snow-storm. It was Byrom's "Divine Pastoral:"

> The Lord is my shepherd, my guardian and guide;
> Whatsoever I want he will kindly provide,
> Ever since I was born, it is he that hath crowned
> The life that he gave me with blessings all round.
>
> . . . .
>
> Thro' my tenderest years, with as tender a care,
> My soul like a lamb in his bosom he bare;
> To the brook he would lead me, whene'er I had need
> And point out the pasture where best I might feed.
>
> . . . .
>
> The Lord is my shepherd; what then shall I fear?
> What danger can frighten me whilst he is near?
> Not when the time calls me to walk through the vale
> Of the Shadow of Death shall my heart ever fail;
> Tho' afraid, of myself, to pursue the dark way
> Thy rod and thy staff be my comfort and stay,
> For I know by thy guidance, when once it is past,
> To a fountain of life it will lead me at last.

IN WAR TIME

She sang it to the cheerful tune of Hinton, as oft before when Parson Page had given it out from the pulpit of Goshen church, and she and Abram sat side by side singing from the weather-beaten hymnal that lay now near the Bible on the centre-table. I took it up and turned its yellow pages, wondering at the queer "buckwheat" notes and reading the names of the old church music, "Federal Street," whose tones beat the air like the wing of a tired and home-sick angel; "Windham," that holds in its minor strains the melancholy wails of an autumn wind; "Brattle Street," whose rich full chords are like a confession of faith, — all those old tunes that have grown richer and sweeter by carrying heavenward on the wings of song the devotion of worshipping souls.

Suddenly Aunt Jane's voice ceased in the middle of a word. I looked up. She was sitting motionless, holding in her hand a piece of rusty iron and gazing at it with tragic eyes. As she gazed, that which had been its sheath fell from it in flakes, and there before us, wasted to half its size by the dampness of years, was the dull ghost of a bayonet that once had glittered in the sun's rays on many a southern battle field.

"It's that old bayonet," she said, slowly and sadly.

THE LAND OF LONG AGO

"I ricollect the day Abram plowed it up and brought it to the house. The soldiers camped all around our place durin' the war, and to this day you can't run a furrow without turnin' up a minie-ball or an old canteen or somethin' o' the sort to carry you back to war times and make your heart ache for days to come."

She ran her finger slowly down the bayonet, laying it against the point, while the lines in her face deepened under the shadow of bitter memories.

"To think," she said at last, "that human bein's made in the image o' God, men and brothers, would make a thing like this to use against each other! The longer I live, child, the stranger that war seems to me. I couldn't understand it before it come nor while it was goin' on, and now, after all these years, it's jest as mysterious as it ever was. You know it begun in the spring, the war did, and there's a certain kind o' spring wind and the way the air smells that takes me back to the day when the news come to Goshen that Fort Sumter'd been fired on; and if I was to live to be as old as Methuselah, I don't reckon there'd ever be a spring that wouldn't bring back the spring of '61.

"The comin' of war is a curious thing, child. You

IN WAR TIME

know how it is when you're sittin' in the house or on the porch of a summer's day doin' some piece o' work and thinkin' about nothin' but that work, and the sun'll be shinin' out doors and everything pretty and peaceful, and all at once you'll look up and notice that it's gittin' dark, and you'll hear a little thunder away off yonder in the hills, and before you're ready for it, why the storm's broke and the rain's beatin' in at the windows and doors and the wind's blowin' through the house and carryin' everything before it. Well, that's the way the war come. You've seen the seal o' this State, haven't you, child? — two men standin' together holdin' each other's hands, and the motto around 'em: 'United we stand; divided we fall.' Well, that's jest the way it was in Kentucky before the war come and sp'iled it all. Kentuckians stood together and loved each other, and nobody ever thought they could be divided. But all of a sudden a change come over everybody. Folks that'd been friendly all their lives stopped speakin' to each other; if two neighbors come together and stopped to talk, there'd be high words between 'em, and they'd both be mad when they parted. Out in our neighborhood, instead o' talkin' about the weather and the crops and folks' health and the sermon they'd heard Sunday and the weddin's that were goin' to be, why, it was nothin' but slavery and secession and union and States' rights, and it looked like there was a two-edged sword in every house.

"Father was mighty fond o' readin'. He took two or three papers, and every Sunday mornin' and on their way back home from town the neighbors'd drop in and hear the news; and any time you'd pass his house you'd see a porch full o' men listenin' to Father readin' a speech that somebody'd made in Congress or in the legislature, and Mother, she'd leave her work and come to the door every now and then and listen and, maybe, put in a word.

"I ricollect hearin' Father talk about Crittenden's big speech, the one made in Congress when he was tryin' to head off the war. Father thought pretty near as much of Crittenden as he did of Clay. There never was a speech o' Crittenden's that he didn't read, and he'd say, 'I'd rather handle words like that man does than to be the King of England; and,' says he, 'it's all jest like he says; Kentucky will stand by the Union and die by the Union.' Says he, 'She couldn't do otherwise without goin' back on her own word, and that word's cyarved in stone too. There it is,' says he, ' on the block o' marble that we sent to help build the monument at Washington:

"' The first state to enter the union will be the last to leave it.'

"Says he, 'We can't go back on that word.'

"And then he turns around to Mother and says he, 'Deborah, what do you think about it?' I can see Mother now. She'd been fryin' some meat, and she turned around with the fork in her hand and looked at Father a minute before she answered him, and says she, 'What's the use in askin' me what I think? I'm nothin' but a woman, and what a woman thinks is of mighty little importance.' Says she, 'You men have got this thing in your own hands, and us women, we'll have to put up with whatever comes.'

"I'll never forgit the day Father come from town with the speech that Crittenden made at Lexin'ton right after Fort Sumter'd been taken. It was April, and jest such a day as this, the flowers all comin' up and the sky blue and the bees hummin' around the water maples, and it didn't look as if there could be such a thing as a war comin'. I was at Mother's that day helpin' her take a quilt out o' the frame. Father come in, and old Uncle Haley Pearson, my great-uncle, with him, and they set down on the porch and Father read the speech out loud, stoppin' every now and then to explain somethin' to Uncle Haley, and when he got through Uncle Haley says: 'Well, as near as I can make it out, Crittenden wants us to stand still betwixt the North and the South and try to make 'em keep the peace; and if we can't do that, we're to get on the fence and stay there and watch the fight.' And Father says, 'Yes, that appears to be about the meanin' o' what I've been readin'.' Says he, 'Maybe I don't rightly understand it all, there's so many big words in it, but that's about what I make out of it.'

"Uncle Haley was leanin' over with both hands on his cane, and he shook his head right slow and says he, 'It appears to me that Crittenden ain't as well acquainted with Kentuckians as he might be, and him a Kentuckian and a Senator too.' Says he, 'There ain't a man, or a woman or a child or a yeller dog in Kentucky but what's on one side or the other, and you might as well put two game roosters in the same pen and tell 'em not to fight as to start up a war betwixt the North and the South and tell Kentucky to keep out of it.'

IN WAR TIME

"And Uncle Haley was right about it. The legislature met the very next month and they said jest what Crittenden said, that Kentucky mustn't take sides. But when it come to the p'int o' goin' to the war or stayin' at home and lookin' on, out o' every hundred Kentucky men old enough to go to the war ninety of 'em went on one side or the other. That's the way Kentucky stays out of a fight, honey. I've heard Father say that the war cost Kentucky thirty thousand lives. But that's jest the soldiers; and if you go to countin' the lives that was lost in any war you can't stop with the soldiers. There's my mother; she never saw a battle-field, but the war killed her the same as it did my two brothers."

Here Aunt Jane removed her glasses and leaned back in her chair. By these signs I knew there was to be a digression in the course of the story.

"I wish I could make you see jest what kind of a woman Mother was," she said thoughtfully. "Every generation's different appearin' from the one that comes before it and the one that comes after it. I'm my mother's own child. Folks used to say I had Mother's eyes and Mother's hair, but I'm a mighty different woman from Mother. And my daughters are jest as

THE LAND OF LONG AGO

different from me, and as for my granddaughters, why, you wouldn't know they was any kin to me. I'm a plain old woman and my granddaughters are fine ladies. My grandmother, you know, was the old pioneer stock, and Mother was her oldest child, and she was somethin' like the pioneer women herself. I ricollect when I was at that meetin' of clubs in Lexin'ton, the time I went to see Henrietta, one lady got up and said that a woman ought to be somethin' besides a mother. I reckon that's right for this day and generation, but if you'll go back to my mother's day and my grandmother's day, you'll find that if a woman was a mother then, she didn't have time to be anything else. Bringin' a family o' children into the world and takin' care of 'em, cookin' for 'em, sewin' for 'em and spinnin' and weavin' the cloth for their clothes — that's the way Mother did. She was jest a mother, but that was enough. You know that Bible text, ' Greater love hath no man than this, that he lay down his life for his friend.' I always think o' that text when I think o' the old-time mothers; they had to give up their lives for their children.

"Mother's name was Deborah, and I always thought that name suited her. She was taller and stronger than the common run o' women, and Father used to laugh and say he believed she was half sister o' the Deborah in the Bible, the one that judged Israel, and that was 'A mother in Israel.' Father always looked up to Mother and asked her advice about things, and, as for us children, Mother's word was our law. She ruled us and judged us like the Deborah in the Bible, but I can look back now and see that there never was any love greater than my mother's love for her children. Of course a mother, if she's the right kind of a mother, will love all her children jest because they're hers. But then, over and above that sort o' love, she'll love each one on account o' somethin' that it is or somethin' that it does, and that way every child has a different sort o' love, and maybe one child 'll have a little bit more love than the rest. We always accused Mother of bein' partial to my two brothers, Jonathan and David, and Mother never denied it. She'd laugh and say, ' Well, what if I am? The rest of you ain't mistreated, are you?' And when I ricollect how brother David and brother Jonathan looked and what kind o' men they were, I can't blame Mother for bein' a little prouder and a little fonder o' them than she was o' the rest of us. Mother always called 'em her twins, because there was jest a little over a year betwixt 'em and mighty little difference in their size. David was the oldest, and Mother named him for her father; and when Jonathan was born she said, 'Now, I've got a Jonathan for my David. And,' says she, 'Maybe they'll be good boys and love each other like David and Jonathan did.' You ricollect what the Bible says: 'The soul of Jonathan was knit with the soul of David; and Jonathan loved him as his own soul,' and when Jonathan was killed you ricollect how David said, 'Thy love to me was wonderful, passing the love of woman.'

"And sure enough, child, that's the way it was with my two brothers. Their souls appeared to be knit together, and they loved each other with a love 'passin' the love of woman.'

"The rest of us children used to fall out now and then, like children will, even when they love each other, but David and Jonathan — why, there never was a cross word or hard feelin' between 'em, and it was the prettiest sight in the world to see them two boys walkin' together holdin' each other's hands and laughin' and talkin' like sweethearts. I ricollect once they was sittin' on a bench readin' out o' the same book, and Mother

IN WAR TIME

looked at 'em awhile, and says she to Father, ' Do you reckon there's anything in this world that can ever come betwixt David and Jonathan?' And Father he laughed, and says he, ' Yes, there's one thing that can come betwixt any two men God ever made.' And Mother says, ' What is it?' And Father laughed again — he always liked to tease Mother — and says he, ' Why, a woman, of course.' Says he, ' Jest let them two boys fall in love with the same woman and that'll put a stop to all this David and Jonathan business.'

"But it wasn't a woman that come between my brothers, it was the war. It was a long time before the family found out that David and Jonathan didn't think alike about States' rights; and when we did find out, we paid mighty little attention to it, for we thought they'd come to an agreement about this jest as they had about every other question that'd ever come up between 'em. But when the President made his first call for soldiers, David and Jonathan both went to Mother and asked her consent to enlist. They was of age and might 'a' done as they pleased. But as long as one of us children stayed under Father's roof, we never took a step of any importance that we didn't first ask Mother's consent.

THE LAND OF LONG AGO

"Well, Mother looked at 'em awhile, standin' before her so tall and strong and handsome, and she says, 'My sons, you'll never have my consent to goin' in the army.' And David and Jonathan looked at each other, and then David spoke. 'Well, Mother,' says he, 'if you won't give your consent, we'll have to go without it.' And Mother says, 'You boys never disobeyed me in your lives, are you goin' to disobey me at this late day?' And David says, 'No, Mother, we're goin' to obey you,' says he. 'You've told us from our youth up that we must listen to the voice of conscience and do whatever we thought was right, — I think one way about this matter and Jonathan thinks the other, but we're both listenin' to the voice of conscience and doin' what we think is right jest as you taught us to do.'

"Well, of course, Mother couldn't answer that, and so the word went out that David and Jonathan was goin' to enlist, and all the married brothers and sisters gethered at the old home place to say farewell to 'em.

"Maybe you know, child, how you feel the mornin' after there's been a death in the house. It hardly seems worth while to do any thing, for your heart's in the coffin in the dark room, but you go on and cook

IN WAR TIME

and put the house in order and try to eat the same as if nothin' had happened. And that's the way we all felt the mornin' my brothers went to the war. Mother wouldn't let anybody help her cook breakfast. Says she, ' It's the last thing I can do for my boys, and I don't want any help.' So she cooked the breakfast and waited on the boys and watched 'em while they eat, the same as she'd been doin' all their lives. And when the meal was over, Father was at the gate with the wagon to take 'em to town to catch the mornin' train to Louisville, and from there Jonathan had to go to Camp Joe Holt over in Indiana — that's where the Federals had their recruitin' place — and David, he was to go to Camp Boone in Tennessee. All of us went out to the gate to say farewell, and there wasn't a tear dropped nor a useless word said. If one had cried we'd all 'a' cried. But we saw that Mother was holdin' her tears back, so we all did the same. And we stood and looked till the wagon was out o' sight, and then everybody went back to the house feelin' as if we'd jest come back from a buryin'. Well, from that day on, all we lived for was to hear the news from the battles and find out which side beat. Some o' the neighbors was on the side o' the North and some on

THE LAND OF LONG AGO

the side o' the South, and one could rejoice to-day and another one to-morrow, and one was prayin' for Lee and the other for Grant, but Mother she'd say, ' It's all one! It's all one! There's no rejoicin' for me no matter which side wins, and the only prayer I can pray is " Lord! Lord! put an end to this war and give me back my boys."' People used to come over and talk to Mother and try to make her see things different. Uncle Haley says to her once, says he, ' Deborah, can't you think o' your country? There's a great question to be settled. Nobody knows which is the strongest, the government up yonder at Washin'ton, or the government down yonder in South Carolina and right here in Kentucky. It's a big question,' says he, ' and it's been botherin' this country ever since it's been a country, and this war's goin' to settle it one way or the other for good and all, and no matter which side a man's fightin' on, he's doin' his part in the settlement.' Says he, ' You've got a son on each side, and you ought to feel proud and glad that you're doin' so much for your country.' And Mother's eyes'd flash and she'd say, ' Country! You men never told me I had a country till you got up this war and took my sons away from me. I'm nothin' but a poor old woman that's spent her life raisin' up a family, and what's a country to me unless I've got my sons?'"

The mother-heart! It beats to the same measure, be it Garibaldi's time in Italy or war-time in Kentucky.

> And when Italy's made, for what end is it done
> If we have not a son?
>
> . . . .
>
> When you have your country from mountain to sea,
> When King Victor has Italy's crown on his head.
> (And I have my dead.)

"If David and Jonathan had been on the same side," continued Aunt Jane, "it would 'a' been easier for Mother; but she used to say it was like havin' her heart torn in two, and one half of it was with David and the other half with Jonathan, and she worried herself nearly crazy over the fear that one of her boys might kill the other. And the fightin' kept on, the battles longer and harder all the time, — Manassas and Fort Donaldson and Pea Ridge and Mill Spring, and there was hardly a time when it wasn't Kentuckian against Kentuckian, and at last come the battle o' Shiloh."

On that fatal word Aunt Jane's voice broke. She

THE LAND OF LONG AGO

turned away from me and covered her face with her apron, and there was a long pause. The rains of more than forty springs had cleansed the earth from the taint of blood; grass and flowers and grain were growing over the old battle-field; but, like the wand of a wizard, the rusty bayonet had waved out of sight and out of mind the decades of peace, and her tears flowed for a grief too deep to be healed by the flight of mortal years.

Presently, with trembling hands she began arranging the boxes and bundles on the shelves. There were no unfinished tasks in Aunt Jane's life; the closet must be cleaned, and a story once begun must be told to the end. She steadied her voice and went on.

"You know, honey," she said, "the battle o' Shiloh lasted two days and the evenin' of the first day a curious thing happened. Mother was stayin' with me, for Father was with the home gyards, and in them days the women had to huddle up together and protect each other the best they could. I was in the kitchen cookin' supper, and Mother was in the front room sittin' in her old rockin' chair by the winder lookin' out at the pretty sky, when the sun had about gone

"'DAVID! JONATHAN! MY BOYS! WHERE ARE YOU?'"
Page 257.

down. I could hear her rockin' and the old chair creakin'. Pretty soon it got so dark I couldn't see what I was doin', and I lit a candle, and jest as I was settin' it on the shelf above the table, I heard Mother give a cry and go runnin' to the front door. I picked up the candle and went out to see what was the matter, but as I opened the door o' the front room a gust o' wind blew out the candle, and I run out in the dark, and there was Mother standin' in the door leanin' forward as if she was lookin' and listenin', and before I could git to her she rushed out on the porch and around the house callin' 'David! Jonathan! My boys! Where are you?'

"I thought certain Mother had lost her mind, and I went after her and caught her by the arm, and, says I, 'Mother, what on earth's the matter? Come back in the house; you're gittin' your feet all wet with the dew.' And she jerked away from me and went on clear around the house lookin' in every dark place under the trees and the vines and callin' her boys. And when she got to the front door again, she stopped and said to me, 'Jane, didn't you hear the foot-steps?' And I says, 'What foot-steps, Mother?' and she says, 'Why, Jonathan and David's, of course.' Says she,

THE LAND OF LONG AGO

'I heard 'em comin' up the front walk jest like I've heard 'em a hundred times before, comin' in from the field at night.' And she started around the house again, and says she, 'May be they're hidin' out somewhere tryin' to surprise me.'

" Well, it was the longest time before I could persuade Mother to come in, and all the evenin' she talked about the footsteps and how plain they sounded, and every now and then she'd go to the door and look and listen and call their names.

" God only knows what she heard, but the next day we got news of the fightin' at Shiloh, and David was there with General Johnston, and Jonathan, he was with Grant. "

She turned away, and again there was a long silence. To me who listened the war was but a story on a printed page, but to her who told the tale, it was a chapter of life written in tears and blood, and better for Aunt Jane if the old bayonet had lain forever in the soil of the far field. But again she took up the story.

" I've heard folks say, child, that the funeral's the saddest thing about a death; but it's a sadder thing to have a death without a funeral.

IN WAR TIME

"You ricollect me tellin' you about that picture I saw at Henrietta's, 'The Angelus?' Well, there was another picture I'll never forgit as long as I live. It was a picture of Rizpah. I reckon you know who Rizpah was; you ought to know, any how."

Aunt Jane looked inquiringly at me and paused for a reply. Rizpah? Rizpah? Yes, somewhere I had heard that stately name, but where? Was it in Greece or Rome or France or Italy? Juliet I knew, and Octavia and Iphigenia and Aspasia —

Had Rizpah any kinship to these? Aunt Jane's eyes were searching my face.

"Honey," she said gravely, "you might jest as well own up that you don't know who Rizpah was. That comes o' parents not makin' their children read the Scriptures. When I was a child we had to read our Bibles every Sunday evenin' till pretty near sundown. I can't say we enjoyed it much, but when we grew up we didn't have to blush for shame when anybody asked us a Bible question. Now, you take my Bible yonder on the table, and find the second book of Samuel. I can't be expected to ricollect exactly the chapter or the verse, but you look around in that book till you see Rizpah's name and then read what it says."

THE LAND OF LONG AGO

I made a hasty search for the passage and presently found it:

"But the King took the two sons of Rizpah, the daughter of Aiah, whom she bare unto Saul, Armoni and Mephibosheth; and the five sons of Michal the daughter of Saul, whom she brought up for Adriel the son of Barzillai the Meholathite; and he delivered them into the hands of the Gibeonites, and they hanged them in the hill before the Lord: and they fell all seven together, and were put to death in the days of harvest, in the first days, in the beginning of barley harvest.

"And Rizpah, the daughter of Aiah, took sackcloth, and spread it for her upon the rock, from the beginning of harvest until the water dropped upon them out of heaven, and suffered neither the birds of the air to rest on them by day, nor the beasts of the field by night."

"There!" said Aunt Jane, "that's Rizpah. Now try to remember that story, child. You couldn't help rememberin' it if you'd ever seen the picture. It was an awful thing to look at, but somehow if you looked at it once you couldn't help goin' back to it again. There was the sky and the light breakin' through the clouds. I never could tell whether it was right after sundown or jest before sunrise — and the dead bodies hangin' from the limbs o' the trees, stiff and straight, and Rizpah fightin' off the vultures with a club, her long black hair streamin' down her back and her eyes blazin' like coals of fire. The minute I looked at that picture, I says to myself, 'That's Mother.' Many a night she'd dream of seein' the bodies of her sons lyin' on the battle-field and the birds pickin' the flesh from their bones, and she'd wake up cryin' and wring her hands and say, 'If I could only know that their bodies was buried safe in the ground, I could stand it better.' But we never did know, and — it's a curious thing, honey — when you don't see the dead buried you never can be right sure that they ain't alive yet somewhere or other on this earth.

"The footsteps never come again, but all her life Mother listened for 'em, and I hope and trust that when she got to the other side, the first thing she heard was the steps of her boys comin' towards her jest like they used to come before the war parted 'em."

She dried her eyes once more on the gingham apron and tried to smile at me in her usual way, but the smile would not come.

THE LAND OF LONG AGO

"This ain't the right kind of a story to tell you, honey, on a pretty spring day," she said brokenly, "and I never set out to tell it. But that old bayonet got me started, and before I knew it I was right back in war times livin' it all over. And while I'm about it, there's one more story I'm goin' to tell you, whether you want to hear it or not. It's about Elizabeth Taylor. I reckon I've told you Sally Ann's experience, haven't I? And if you ricollect that, you'll know who Elizabeth Taylor was.

"Elizabeth felt different from Mother about the war. She was strong for States' rights, and when Harrison, the only son she had, went into the army, he went with her blessin' and consent, and he made a mighty brave soldier, too. I ricollect the day 'Lizabeth come over to tell us about Harrison bein' promoted at the battle o' Port Gibson. You've heard o' the battle o' Port Gibson, haven't you, honey? That was another time when they fought all day long. I've heard Harrison say the first gun was fired before daylight, and when they give up and begun fallin' back, it was gittin' on towards dusk. Harrison said his officers went down one by one, first the captain and then the lieutenants, and when the last one fell, he up and took charge o' things

IN WAR TIME

himself jest like he'd seen the captain do; and when they found they had to give up the fight, Harrison somehow or other managed to carry away two cannons out o' the six they'd been workin' that day, and with these two he kind o' kept the Yankees off while the men fell back, and if it hadn't been for that they'd 'a' been cut all to pieces. Harrison was nothin' but a striplin', not out of his teens, but he went into that battle a sergeant and he come out of it a captain. 'Lizabeth was the proudest, gladdest woman you ever saw; says she, ' I've had a hard life, but this pays me for all my troubles.'

" But what I set out to tell you was somethin' 'Lizabeth herself did, not what Harrison did. It was along towards the close of the war, the summer of '64. One evenin' in July a squad o' Yankee soldiers come gallopin' along the pike about dark, and camped over in the fields back of 'Lizabeth's house. 'Lizabeth said she went up in the garret and looked out o' the window, and she could see 'em lightin' their camp-fires and feedin' their horses and cookin' supper. There wasn't a soul on the place with her except old Aunt Dicey and Uncle Jake. 'Lizabeth's brother was a slave owner, and when Harrison went to the war he sent

THE LAND OF LONG AGO

Aunt Dicey and her husband over to 'Lizabeth's to watch over her and keep her company.

"Well, that night 'Lizabeth said she didn't feel much like sleepin', not knowin' but what the soldiers might come at any minute to search the house or maybe set it on fire. But she said her prayers and was almost fallin' off to sleep when she happened to think of some powder that Harrison had hid over in that field. Harrison was mighty fond of huntin', and always kept a big supply o' powder on hand, and the day before he went to the war he carried the can over to that field and hid it in a holler tree. 'For,' says he, 'I don't propose to be furnishin' ammunition to the Yankees.' 'Lizabeth said her heart stopped beatin' when she thought o' that powder and the fires all around, and the ground covered with dry grass and leaves. And she thought, 'Suppose the grass and leaves should catch a fire and the fire spread to the tree,' and she got up and put on her clothes and went to the garret again and looked out o' the window, and she could see a fire right near where she thought the old holler tree was standin', and her conscience says to her, 'If anybody's killed by that powder blowin' up whose fault will it be?' She said she knew she

IN WAR TIME

ought to go and git the powder, but the very thought o' that made her shake from head to foot. And she went back to bed and tried to sleep, but when she shut her eyes all she could see was a fire spreadin' amongst the leaves and grass and creepin' up to an old holler tree, and she thought how every one o' them soldiers lyin' there asleep had a mother and maybe a wife and a sister that was prayin' for 'em. And all at once somethin' said to her, 'Suppose it was your boy in this sort o' danger; wouldn't you thank any woman that'd go to his help?' And then she saw in a minute that there wasn't but one thing for her to do: she must go and take that powder out o' the holler tree and put it out o' the reach o' fire. So she threw an old shawl over her head and went out to the cabin and called Uncle Jake, and asked him to go with her across the field betwixt the house and the place where the soldiers had their camp. The old man was no manner o' protection, for he was so crippled up with rheumatism that he had mighty little use of his feet and hands, but 'Lizabeth said she felt a little bit safer havin' some human bein' along with her crossin' that big field.

"The moon was about in its third quarter that

THE LAND OF LONG AGO

night, and 'Lizabeth said if the sentries had been awake they could 'a' seen her and Uncle Jake creepin' through the high weeds in the field. And every now and then she'd stop and listen, and then go on a little piece and stop and listen again, and that way they got to the far corner of the field, and Uncle Jake he crouched down behind a big oak stump, and she crawled under the bars o' the fence, and there was the fires all burnin' low, but givin' enough light along with the moon to keep her from stumblin' over the soldiers lyin' asleep on the ground. She said she gethered her skyirts around her and picked her way to the holler tree and pulled the powder out and put it in the skyirt of her dress and started back. She said she was so skeered she never stopped to see whether there really was any danger of fire spreadin' to the tree and settin' off the powder. She had jest one thought in her mind, and that was to git the powder and go back home.

"Did you ever dream, child, of tryin' to go somewhere and your feet feelin' as if they had weights on 'em and you couldn't move 'em? Well, 'Lizabeth said that was the way she felt when she started back to the fence with that powder. It was mighty heavy and weighted her down, so that she had to walk slow, and she could hear the soldiers breathin', and once one of 'em said somethin' in his sleep, and she come pretty near faintin' from fright. Every step seemed like a mile, and she thought she never would git back to the fence. But God watched over her, and she got out o' the camp and back to the house safe and sound. She said when she stepped up on her back porch she felt like a weight as heavy as the powder had been taken off her conscience, and she went up stairs and kneeled down and thanked God for givin' her courage to do the right thing, and then she went to bed and slept as peaceful as a child.

"Now, you may think, child, that 'Lizabeth put on her bonnet and come over and told me this the day after it happened; but she didn't. 'Lizabeth never was any hand to talk about herself, and it was an accident that anybody ever heard what she'd done. I happened to be at her house one day, maybe six months or so after the war was over, and Harrison was searchin' around in the closet, pullin' things out like I've been doin' to-day, and he come across the powder. He looked at it a minute, and says he, 'Why, here's that powder I hid in the old holler tree; I'd clean forgot it. How did it get here, Mother?' And 'Lizabeth says, 'Why, son, I went and got it the night the Yankees camped over in the woods at the back o' the house.' Harrison looked at her like he thought she was talkin' out of her head, and says he, 'What did you say, Mother?' And 'Lizabeth went on to tell him jest what I've told you, as unconcerned as if she was tellin' about walkin' from the front door to the front gate. And when she got through, Harrison drew a long breath, and says he, 'Mother, I'm proud of you! That's braver than anything I ever did. They made me a captain, but you ought to be a general.' And 'Lizabeth, she colored up, and says she, 'Why, son, any woman that had the heart of a mother in her would 'a' done jest what I did. It's nothin' to make any fuss over.'

"I ain't overly fond o' tellin' stories about war times, child," concluded Aunt Jane, "but I like to tell this, for it's somethin' that ought to be ricollected. Harrison showed me a big book once, The Ricords of the Rebellion, and his name as big as life on one o' the pages, tellin' how he was promoted twice in one day; but 'Lizabeth outlived her husband and all her children, and you won't find so much as a stone to

IN WAR TIME

mark her grave, and in a little while nobody'll ever know that such a woman as 'Lizabeth Taylor ever lived; yet, it's jest as Harrison said; what she did was braver than anything he did. And it's my belief that Harrison never would 'a' been the soldier he was if he hadn't had his mother's conscience. It was 'Lizabeth's conscience that made her stand up in church and own up to usin' our Mite Society money, and made her leave her bed that night and risk her life for the lives o' them soldier boys, and it was her conscience in her son that kept him at his post on the field o' battle when everybody else was runnin' off; and that's why 'Lizabeth's name ought to be ricollected along with Harrison's."

"Poor human nature," we sometimes say, forgetting that through every character runs a vein of gold. Now and then kindly chance rends the base earth that covers it and shows us a hero or a heroine. But revealed or unrevealed, all human nature is rich in the possibility of greatness.

Here and there we build a monument; but if for every deed of noble daring some memorial were raised, earth's monuments would be as the stars of heaven or the sands of the sea; the names of the lowly and the great would stand side by side; and the name of the mother by the name of the son. For the valor of man is a mighty stream that all may see as it rolls through the ages, changing the face of the world, but ofttimes its source is a spring of courage rising silently from the secret depths of an unknown woman's heart.

IX
THE WATCH-MEETING

IX

THE WATCH-MEETING

IT was the thirty-first of December. The short winter day had ended in a golden sunset, and the old year was passing in a night of stars. Aunt Jane and I stood on the porch looking westward at the clear wintry sky, where the radiance from the silver lamp of Venus gleamed as clearly over the bare, frozen earth as if it were lighting the feet of lovers through the rose-

THE LAND OF LONG AGO

gardens of June. All the winds of heaven were sleeping, and the cold still air was like a draught from a mountain spring. Our eyes were on the same star, but our thoughts were far apart; mine with the years to come, and Aunt Jane's with the years that were past.

"Fine night for a watch-meetin'," she remarked at last.

"A watch-meeting?" I queried. "What is a watch-meeting?"

Aunt Jane turned her face toward me, and through the darkness I felt her look of deep reproach. "Child," she said gravely, "do you mean to tell me that you don't know what a watch-meetin' is, and you livin' in a Christian country all your life? Next thing you'll be tellin' me you don't know what a prayer-meetin' is. However, I don't know as you're to blame. Your grandfather and grandmother went to watch-meetin', and your mother knows what it is, but I reckon watch-meetin's are as much out o' fashion these days as purple caliker dresses and turkey-tail fans. In my day, child, folks went to church New-year's eve and sung and prayed the old year out and the new year in, and that's a watch-meetin'."

"How interesting!" I exclaimed.

THE WATCH-MEETING

Aunt Jane chuckled softly. "Yes, it was mighty interestin'," she said, "and there was one watch-meetin' I'll never forget as long as I live. But you come into the house. This ain't the weather for old folks or young folks either to be standin' out on the porch."

We went in, and I laid a stick of wood on the andirons in the open fireplace. A momentary splendor lit the room as the gray moss and lichens caught fire and the swift flames ran from one end of the log to the other and then died out, while the smoke from the kindling wood rose in the huge chimney.

"There's never a New-year's eve that I don't think o' that watch-meetin'," Aunt Jane continued, "and I set here and laugh to myself over the times we used to have in the old Goshen church. Jest hand me my knittin', child, and I'll tell you about that meetin'. It's jest as easy to talk as it is to think."

The room was lighted only by the faint glow from the fireplace, but Aunt Jane needed no lamp or candle to guide her through the maze of stitches in the heel of the gray stocking. I sat with folded hands and wondered at the deft fingers that wove the yarn into the web of the stocking, and at the deft brain that, from the thread of old memories, could weave the web of

THE LAND OF LONG AGO

a story in which was caught and held the spirit of an older day.

"The night o' that watch-meetin'," began Aunt Jane, "was jest such a night as this, cold and clear and still; and if you're wrapped up well and have a good warm quilt over your knees, why, it's nothin' but a pleasure to ride a mile or so to the church. A watch-meetin' is different from any other church-meetin'. It generally comes on a week-day, it ain't preachin' and it ain't prayer-meetin', and you don't have to remember to keep the day holy; so you can laugh and talk goin' and comin' and before the meetin' begins. Next to a May-meetin' a watch-meetin's about the pleasantest sort of a church-meetin' there is.

"Now, as you didn't know what a watch-meetin' is, it ain't likely you know what a May-meetin' is, either. There, now! I knew you wouldn't. Well, child, that all comes o' livin' in town. Town's a fine place to go to once in a while, but there's a heap o' disadvantages about livin' there all the time. A May-meetin' is the first Sunday in May, when we all take big baskets o' dinner to the church and eat out-doors under the trees after preachin's over. And now

THE WATCH-MEETING

let me git back to my story or, the first thing you know, I'll be tellin' about a May-meetin' instead of a watch-meetin'. But I thought I'd better explain it to you right now, honey, so's you won't be mortified this way again. There's some things everybody's expected to know, and this is one of 'em.

"I ricollect jest how the old church looked the night o' that watch-meetin'. It was soon after we'd got the new organ, and the shine hadn't wore off the new cyarpet yet, and the lamps was burning bright on the stands each side o' the pulpit and on the organ. Some o' the young folks had hung branches o' pine and cedar around the walls and over the winders, and you could hear the hickory wood cracklin' and poppin' in the stove at the back o' the church, and there was all the Goshen folks sittin' in their pews: Sam and Milly, and Hannah and Miles, and Maria and Silas, and Uncle Jim and Sally Ann, and Parson Page down in front o' the pulpit leanin' back in his chair with his chin restin' on his hand and his other hand proppin' up his elbow. The young folks of course was in the back part o' the church, where they could talk and laugh without bein' seen by their parents; and little Sam Amos and two or three more o' the Goshen boys,

THE LAND OF LONG AGO

along with Martin Luther Wilson, was sittin' down on the pulpit steps, where they could see everything that was to be seen and hear everything that was to be heard."

Aunt Jane began to laugh gently, and the knitting dropped from her hands. Another moment and she would have slipped away to the watch-meeting of forty years ago, leaving me alone in the quiet shadow-haunted room; but I called her back.

"How did Martin Luther happen to be at Goshen?" I asked. It was an idle question, but it served my purpose.

"Why, don't you ricollect?" said Aunt Jane brightly. "Brother Wilson preached in town, but after Squire Schuyler give him that house for a weddin' fee he lived there. That was betwixt and between the town and the country. Martin Luther loved the country jest like his father did, and there never was a watch-meetin' or a May-meetin' that Martin Luther wasn't on hand; but I'm bound to say that most o' the time it wasn't for any good.

"Well, by nine o'clock everything was ready for the watch-meetin' to begin, and Parson Page set the clock on the floor back o' the pulpit — it sounds a heap

THE WATCH-MEETING

solemner at a watch-meetin', child, to hear the clock strike when you can't see it — and then he give out the first hymn:

> " ' A few more years shall roll,
> A few more seasons come,
> And we shall be with those that rest,
> Asleep within the tomb.

> " ' A few more suns shall set
> O'er these dark hills of time,
> And we shall be where suns are not,
> A far serener clime.' "

To me there seemed nothing joy-inspiring in the old hymn, but Aunt Jane smiled radiantly as she chanted the melancholy words that held in their cadences the voices of the choir and the music of the organ in the old country church.

"That's one o' the hymns we always sung at a watch-meetin'," she observed, " that and

> " ' Lo, on a narrow neck of land
> 'Twixt two unbounded seas I stand.'

"I love every one o' the old hymns, child, jest as much as I love my Bible, and I can take that hymn-book yonder and read over the hymns we used to sing

THE LAND OF LONG AGO

at prayer-meetin' and communion and funerals and baptizin's, and I declare it's jest like livin' over again all the Sundays of my life. When we got through singin' the hymn Parson Page read a chapter out o' the Bible. It was the ninetieth psalm, the one that begins, 'Lord, thou hast been our dwelling place in all generations'; and then he give us a little talk, not a sermon exactly, but jest a little talk about the new year and the old year. I ricollect pretty much all he said as well as if it was yesterday. He said that there was nothin' sad about the passin' of the years, and every New-year's eve ought to be a time for rejoicin'; that life was jest a gainin' and a losin' and the two balanced pretty even. Every year we lost a little of our youth and a little of our strength, but we gained in wisdom and understandin'. He said if we'd improved our time and come up to our opportunities durin' the past year, we could go forward joyfully to meet the new year, and if we hadn't, why, still there wasn't any reason for givin' up and feelin' downhearted, for the mercy of the Lord was infinite, and there was always another chance waitin' for us, and if a man turned over a new leaf and made up his mind to do better, every day was a New-year's day.

THE WATCH-MEETING

"And then he called on the men folks to tell what their experience had been durin' the past year, and jest as Uncle Jim Mathews got up to tell his experience the clock struck ten, and Uncle Jim says: 'Brethren, you hear that? Jest two more hours of this year is left to us.' Says he, 'I don't know how it is with the rest of you, but for my part I feel that this has been a profitable year for my soul. I feel,' says he, 'that I have grown in grace and in the knowledge of the Lord, that my faith has been strengthened, that patience has had her perfect work in me, and that I'm nearer to the kingdom than I ever was'; and he went on this way for about ten minutes, and Sally Ann whispered to me and says she, 'If one-half o' that's true, the Lord ought to send down a chariot of fire and take Uncle Jim up to heaven this very night.'

"Then Uncle Jerry Amos got up and says he, 'Brethren, I thank the Lord that during the past year I have grown more charitable toward my fellow men.' And to save our lives we couldn't help laughin' at that, for if there was anything Uncle Jerry didn't need it was more charity. I ricollect when old man Abner Simpson died — he was a mighty mean man, so mean that Parson Page had a heap o' trouble to preach the right kind of a funeral sermon about him — and right after the funeral Uncle Jerry heard some o' the neighbors talkin' about him and says he: 'Boys, ain't you ashamed to be talkin' this way about the dead? Don't you know you mustn't say anything but good about the dead, or the livin' either, for that matter?' And Bush Elrod says, 'Now, Uncle Jerry, you know nobody could say anything good about old man Abner; you couldn't yourself.' And Uncle Jerry says: 'Yes, I can. Jest give me time, and I can think o' plenty o' good things to say about him.' And he stood and thought and thought, and the rest o' the men laughin' at him, and Bush Elrod says, 'You'll have to give it up, Uncle Jerry.' But Uncle Jerry says, 'No, there never was a human bein' that somethin' good couldn't be said about him.' And pretty soon he slapped his side and says he: 'I've got it! He had a good appetite.' That's why we all had to laugh when Uncle Jerry said he'd grown more charitable toward his fellow men.

"Well, all the men folks got up and told what progress in grace they'd made durin' the year, and I ricollect Sam Amos sayin' it was astonishin' how many saints there was in Goshen church, but nobody knew anything about 'em till we had an experience-meetin'. After

THE WATCH-MEETING

the experiences had all been give in we sung another hymn and had another prayer. Then the clock struck eleven, and Parson Page said, ' We will spend a little time in forming good resolutions for the coming year.' And after we'd set there a while makin' our resolutions and had some more singin' and prayin', he said, ' Brethren and sisters, let us give the remaining minutes of the old year to silent prayer for grace that will help us to keep the good resolutions we've made for the new year that is so close at hand.' And we all bowed our heads feelin' mighty solemn, everything so still you could hear the folks around you breathin' and the old clock back o' the pulpit tickin', tickin' away the minutes o' the old year. And we set there expectin' every minute to hear the first stroke o' twelve.

"I ricollect Abram had rheumatism in the muscles of his neck that winter, and leanin' over was mighty painful to him; so pretty soon he straightened up, but all the rest of us kept our heads bowed on the back o' the pew in front of us, and waited for the clock to strike. Somehow or other the time seemed mighty long, and everybody begun to feel restless. Sam Amos was in the pew jest across the aisle from me and Abram and I saw him take out his watch and look at it, and

THE LAND OF LONG AGO

Uncle Jim Mathews dropped off to sleep and got to snorin', and that set the young folks to laughin', and everybody got tired leanin' their heads over so long, and every now and then somebody would straighten up, till at last everybody was settin' up straight except two or three that was fast asleep. And still the clock didn't strike, and I reckon we'd 'a' stayed there till daylight if it hadn't been for Sam Amos. Everybody knew there was something wrong, but nobody had the courage to git up and say so except Sam. He rose up in his pew and says he, 'Neighbors, I don't want to disturb this watch-meetin', but it looks to me like one of two things has happened: either the new year's got lost on the way or the old year's took a notion to stay with us a little longer, and,' says he, 'I move that somebody goes behind the pulpit and sees if there ain't somethin' wrong with the clock.'

"Well, Parson Page he got up and went up the pulpit steps — I ricollect he had to step over Martin Luther's legs; Martin Luther was lyin' over on his face sound asleep — and he stooped down and looked at the clock, and then he threw up his hands and says he: 'Why, bless my soul! It's nearly one o'clock.'

"Well, with that the young folks begun to laugh

THE WATCH-MEETING

scandalous, and everybody jumped up and begun talkin' at once. Abram says, 'The strikin' part o' that clock must be out o' fix.' And Parson Page says, 'That can't be, for I carried it to town last week and had it put in order especially for this occasion.' And Milly Amos says, 'Why didn't some o' you men folks look at your watches instead o' lettin' us sit here wastin' all this good time?' And Sam Amos says, 'I did look at mine, but it didn't do much good, for I forgot to wind it last night, and it had stopped at half-past five in the mornin' or the evenin', I couldn't tell which.' And Silas Petty said his watch hadn't been keepin' good time lately, and he didn't think it was worth while to look at it. And Parson Page said he laid his watch on the bureau and forgot to put it back in his vest pocket when he put on his Sunday clothes. And somebody says, 'Maybe the clock struck and we didn't hear it.' And Abram says: 'I'm pretty certain the strikin' part o' that clock is out o' fix. Probably it got jarred bringin' it over here.'

" Jest then the old clock struck one, as loud and clear as you please. And Parson Page says: 'Do you hear that? There's nothing wrong with the clock; it must be our ears that are out of fix.' And Silas Petty says:

THE LAND OF LONG AGO

'There's nothin' the matter with my ears. It's my opinion some o' those rascally boys have been foolin' with the clock jest to play a trick on us. They've had a mighty good chance at it, sprawlin' around here on the floor and the clock out o' sight behind the pulpit.' Little Sam Amos and the Crawford boys they spoke up and says they, 'We never touched the clock,' and Milly says: 'You can't lay it on little Sam. He's been fast asleep for the last two hours.' And somebody says, 'Where's Martin Luther?' and we all looked around, and Parson Page says, 'Why, he must be here; he was sound asleep on the floor when I stepped up here to examine the clock.' And Sam Amos says, 'Look a-yonder, will you?' and he p'inted toward the winder, and there was Martin Luther up on the winder-sill outside, with his face right up against the glass and his nose all flattened out, and grinnin' like a Cheshire cat. And as soon as he saw us lookin' at him, he dropped down to the ground and give a whoop like a wild Indian and went tearin' down the road as hard as he could foot it in the direction of Schuyler Hall.

"Well, honey, it was right aggravatin'. You know country folks have to work hard and git up early, and

THE WATCH-MEETING

there we'd lost a good hour o' sleep all for nothin', and a madder set o' folks you never saw, all but the young folks. They laughed and laughed, and of course that made us all still madder. Silas Petty and Dave Crawford begun blessin' Martin Luther and sayin' what ought to be done to him and how they was goin' to let Brother Wilson know about this as soon as day broke, and Sam Amos he listened to 'em a while and then says he: ' Now here it is, the new year jest an hour old, and you church-members are breakin' every one o' your good resolutions about keepin' your temper and bein' charitable to your neighbors. Can't you make allowances for a boy?' And Uncle Jerry says: ' That's right, Sam. What's the use in takin' notice of a boy's pranks? We've all been boys once — all except the women folks — and there ain't one of us that hasn't rocked houses and stole watermelons and robbed orchards and disturbed meetin' and done all the rest o' the devilment that boys delight in. But jest let a boy play a joke on us and we forgit all about the sins of our youth. To hear us talk, a person would think that we was born sixty years old.' Says he: ' All we've lost is an hour's sleep, and we can make that up by goin' to bed earlier to-morrow night. Now, why not overlook this little caper of Martin Luther's and begin the new year in a good humor with everything and everybody?'

"And Sam Amos he begun to laugh, and he laughed till he had to set down, and he kept on till Milly got skeered and beat him in the back to make him stop, and finally he got his breath and says he, 'I'm laughin' to think how we all looked settin' here at one o'clock in the mornin' waitin' to hear the clock strike twelve.' And then he started out again, and we laughed with him, and everybody went home in a good humor. I ricollect me and Abram had an argument on the way home about whether it was worth while to go to bed or not. Abram said it was worth while to go to bed if you couldn't sleep but a half-hour, but betwixt laughin' and ridin' in the cold air I was so wide awake I felt like I never wanted to sleep again; and I went to work and cleaned up the house and cut out some sewin' and had breakfast ready by half-past four. I never made that sleep up, child, and I never felt any worse for it. You know what the Bible says, 'As thy days so shall thy strength be,' and when a person's young, there's strength for the day and more besides."

THE WATCH-MEETING

Aunt Jane dropped her knitting and rested her head against the patchwork cover of the high-backed chair. Like a great wall of shelter and defense, we felt around us the deep stillness of a midwinter night in the country. The last traveler had gone his homeward way over the pike hours ago, and in the quiet room we could hear now and then those faint noises made by shrinking timbers, as if the old house groaned in the icy clutch of the December cold, and, louder and clearer than by day, the voice of the clock ticking away the last hours of the old year.

What is there in the flight of years to sadden the heart? Our little times and seasons are but fragments of eternity, and eternity is ours. The sunset on which we gaze with melancholy eyes is a sunrise on the other side of the world, and the vanishing days can take from us nothing that may not be restored by some day yet unborn. Eternity! Immortality! If mortal mind could but fathom the depth of these ideas, they would be as wells of peace in which all trouble, all regret, would be forever drowned. But as Aunt Jane and I sat alone by her deserted hearth we saw the shadows of the night deepening while the fire burned low, and in our hearts we felt another and a darker

THE LAND OF LONG AGO

shadow cast by the wing of the passing year. And, breaking our dreams, the clock struck ten. Aunt Jane gave a start, and the ball of yarn fell from her lap. She picked it up before I could reach it, and winding the yarn and rolling the stocking around the ball she called in her wandering thoughts and entered instantly into the life of the present hour.

"Light the lamp, child," she said, "and hand me my Bible. The Scripture's got a word suitable for every season, and I'll read you the psalm that Parson Page read the night the clock didn't strike."

Reverently she laid the heavy calf-bound volume across her knees, and turning the leaves with swift and certain fingers she found the ninetieth psalm as readily as the twentieth-century woman finds Sordello in her complete Browning. Centuries ago, a Hebrew, standing on one of the mountain peaks of old age, saw in a vision the little lives and the little deeds of men outlined against a background of the "eternal years of God." He put the vision into words, and because they held a universal thought, a burden of the soul in every age and clime, those words have outlasted kingdoms and dynasties. I had often heard the rhythmic lines rolling from priestly lips and echo-

"REVERENTLY SHE LAID THE HEAVY CALF-BOUND VOLUME
ACROSS HER KNEES."
Page 290.

THE WATCH-MEETING

ing under cathedral arches, but never had they moved me as now, when by the dying fire in the last hours of a dying year, I heard them, half chanted, half read, in the tremulous voice of an old woman whose feet were on the same height and whose eyes beheld the same vision:

"Lord, thou hast been our dwelling place in all generations.

"Before the mountains were brought forth, or ever thou hadst formed the earth and the world, even from everlasting to everlasting, thou art God.

"Thou turnest man to destruction; and sayest, Return, ye children of men.

"For a thousand years in thy sight are but as yesterday when it is past, and as a watch in the night.

"Thou carriest them away as with a flood; they are as a sleep: in the morning they are like grass which groweth up.

"In the morning it flourisheth, and groweth up; in the evening it is cut down, and withereth. . . .

"For all our days are passed away in thy wrath; we spend our years as a tale that is told.

"The days of our years are threescore years and ten;

THE LAND OF LONG AGO

and if by reason of strength they be fourscore years, yet is their strength labor and sorrow; for it is soon cut off, and we fly away. . . .

"So teach us to number our days, that we may apply our hearts unto wisdom. . . .

"O satisfy us early with thy mercy; that we may rejoice and be glad all our days.

"Make us glad according to the days wherein thou hast afflicted us, and the years wherein we have seen evil.

"Let thy work appear unto thy servants, and thy glory unto their children.

"And let the beauty of the Lord our God be upon us; and establish thou the work of our hands upon us; yea, the work of our hands establish thou it."

Aunt Jane removed her glasses and folded her withered hands over the sacred pages. "You know, child," she said, "the Bible's the word of God. I ain't questionin' that. But it looks like to me there's some o' the words of man in it, too. Now this psalm I've jest read is the very one to read at a watch-meetin' on New-year's eve because it's all about time and life and the passin' o' the years, but there's some o' the

THE WATCH-MEETING

verses I'd like to leave out. There's that tenth one about 'the days of our years' and the strength of our years. I reckon we all feel like sayin' such things when we git tired and it looks like we haven't done the work we set out to do, but that's the sort o' feelin' to keep to ourselves. It don't do any good to tell such feelin's. And when a man can say that the Lord has been his dwellin' place in all generations, he oughtn't to turn right around and say that the strength of his years is jest labor and sorrow. The trouble with some folks is that they're always lookin' back and countin' the years wherein they have seen evil, but they don't ricollect that the Lord's promise is to make us glad accordin' to the evil years. Trouble has got to come to us, child, but whenever it comes we ought to know there's happiness comin' to make up for it jest like this psalm says, 'Make us glad according to the days wherein thou hast afflicted us, and the years wherein we have seen evil.' I've lived pretty near eighty years, and I've had my share o' trouble, but I'm far from sayin' that the strength of my years is nothin' but labor and sorrow. I never had a sorrow that I didn't know there was a happiness comin' to make up for it. I've spent my life 'as a tale that is told,' and I'm

THE LAND OF LONG AGO

nearly to the end of it, but I'd be right glad, child, if I could go back to the beginnin' and have it told all over again."

It is easy to pronounce a benediction on life when life is in its morning; but with the darkness of the long night closing around us the words that rise most often to human lips are the words of the cynic king who, from "the dazzling height of a throne," surveyed the magnificent ruin of his years and said,

"Vanity of vanities; all is vanity."

God once looked at a seething chaos which he called his world and pronounced it good. Only a divinity could do this. And only the divinity in man enables one to look back on the chaos of sorrow, ecstasy, hope, despair, labor, failure, sin, and suffering which we call life and say, "It is all good; I would live it again if I might."

Aunt Jane closed her Bible and laid it on the mahogany centre-table. "Half-past ten o'clock," she said, glancing at the clock in the corner. "I sometimes think, honey, that I'd like to watch the old year out once more, for there's somethin' about the night that the day hasn't got. But I'm too old to lose sleep unless there's a good reason for it, so cover up the fire and

THE WATCH-MEETING

we'll sleep the old year out instead o' watchin' it out. This night's no more'n any other night, and it's jest as Parson Page said, every day's a New-year's day."

By the author of "The Land of Long Ago."

AUNT
JANE OF KENTUCKY

By ELIZA CALVERT HALL

Illustrated by Beulah Strong. 12mo. Cloth. $1.50

Aunt Jane is perfectly delightful. — *The Outlook*, New York.

A book that plays on the heart strings. — *St. Louis Post-Despatch*.

What Mrs. Gaskill did in "Cranford" this author does for Kentucky. — *Syracuse Herald*.

A prose idyl. Nothing more charming has appeared in recent fiction. — MARGARET E. SANGSTER.

These pages have in them much of the stuff that makes genuine literature. — *Louisville Courier Journal*.

Where so many have made caricatures of old-time country folk, Eliza Calvert Hall has caught at once the real charm, the real spirit, the real people, and the real joy of living which was theirs. — *New York Times*.

Have you read that charming little book written by one of your clever Kentucky women — "Aunt Jane of Kentucky" — by Eliza Calvert Hall? It is very wholesome and attractive. Be sure that you read it. — THEODORE ROOSEVELT.

LITTLE, BROWN, & CO., PUBLISHERS
254 WASHINGTON STREET, BOSTON